KV-191-050

LOCOMOTIVES

A picture history

Also available in the same series

MOTOR-CARS: A picture history. Compiled by Colin Munro
AIRCRAFT: A picture history. Compiled by Maurice Allward
SHIPS: A picture history. Compiled by Laurence Dunn

LOCOMOTIVES
A picture history

Series Editor: V. C. Wall, T.D., C.Eng., M.I.Mech.E., F.R.A.S.

Compiled by Brian Reed

A PICCOLO BOOK

PAN BOOKS LTD · LONDON

First published 1970 by Ward Lock Ltd.
This edition published 1971 by Pan Books Ltd.,
33 Tothill Street, London, S.W.1

ISBN 0 330 02875 8

MADE IN ENGLAND
PRINTED IN GREAT BRITAIN
BY BUTLER & TANNER LTD
FROME, SOMERSET

INTRODUCTION

There are still people today in the British Isles who have never travelled on a railway; there are more who have never seen a steam locomotive in regular service. Like the stage-coach before it, the steam locomotive passed into and out of effective existence in little more than 150 years—a very small proportion of the 3,000 years of wheeled vehicles of one kind or another. There are still at least 35,000 steam locomotives in existence throughout the world today (1969), and a few are still being built in India; but the type plays little part now in railway traction, and probably is responsible for well under 10 per cent of all traffic handled. It has been supplanted by diesel and straight electric traction at a rapid rate since 1950.

Though it was the traffic on the ancient colliery waggonways, aided by the long-continued high price of fodder during the Napoleonic wars, that brought forth the steam locomotive to take the place of man and horse, it then became only the practical development of the steam locomotive that made public railways possible.

The steam locomotive had an individuality not approached by electric and diesel types. It was not susceptible to automation or remote control. A poor driver of a main-line diesel locomotive can easily give performance and fuel consumption 5 to 7 per cent worse than those from a good driver, even though both keep time. The difference between a poor crew and a keen and competent crew on a main-line steamer could well be 10 to 15 per cent, and with time recovery thrown in. A good steam crew could get results out of a locomotive in a condition that would have caused a diesel to fold up.

Moreover, while the steam locomotive could be built as a standardised unit just as easily as a diesel or electric locomotive, it did not come at a time when standardised products of low cost and quality were all the rage; and every chief mechanical engineer set about designing and building his own types, believing them to be the best for his own railway, and giving proof of his competence and initiative. Yet the steam locomotive brought chief mechanical engineers and drivers on to one common level in that, in England, the practice of each was always an art and scarcely ever became a science; and in each field there were some consummate artists surrounded by a large number who hardly attained the status of pavement artists.

Though the steam locomotive reached its peaks of efficiency and performance over the years 1930–39, only persons who are past their half-century in age can claim to have known the steam locomotive at its best—when good coal was no more than £1 a ton and one first class passenger paid the coal bill; when labour troubles were few and reasonable; when there was twice as much traffic as there is today; when country towns had no transport other than the railway, the horse and "shanks's pony"; and when all engines were kept beautifully clean and were painted and lined out in marvellous manner, as can be appreciated from some of the illustrations in this book.

As serious forces in railway operation, diesel and electric traction extend over not more than 30 to 40 years, though several important main-line and suburban electrification schemes date back longer. Thus it is that the steam locomotive occupies three-quarters of this book, and the examples range from the very early engines of Trevithick and his immediate successors to those built in numerous countries until after World War II. Fortunately the whole development can also be studied "in the flesh", at the railway museums at Clapham, York, Swindon and South Kensington. Those who visit York should not omit a view of the simple home-made hand tools used by George Stephenson at Killingworth, and marvel at the courage and tenacity of the man who set out to make "travelling engines" by candle light and with such primitive equipment, and whose work over the years 1814–25 made all the later locomotives practicable.

THE STEAM LOCOMOTIVE

As hauling, or tractive, machines, conventional steam locomotives were dependent on the friction between a smooth steel wheel on a smooth steel rail, as electric and diesel locomotives are today. All were of the reciprocating type; that is, the to-and-fro motion of pistons in two or more cylinders was converted to the rotary motion of the wheels by piston rods, crossheads, connecting rods and cranks. At least two cylinders were needed so that the locomotive could always start; and the cranks of the two were at right angles to each other, so that when one cylinder-drive line was on dead centre the other was exerting full power. This direct drive was very simple, because the steam engine could start under load, and its speed and power could be varied infinitely, which is not the case with all other forms of power.

After *Rocket* in 1829 nearly every boiler was of the horizontal multi-tubular type; flames and gas from the firebox at one end were drawn through the tubes to the smokebox by the draught of the exhaust steam, and expelled up the chimney by the blast, giving up their heat to the firebox and tubes as they passed through. On the other side of the thin tubes and firebox plates was the water, converted to steam by the heat. The harder the locomotive worked the more steam passed through the cylinders, the blast became sharper and increased the draught through the tubes, made the fire burn more fiercely and so generated more steam. Temperature in the heart of the firebox could be as much as 2,500 deg. F., and the speed of the gases entering the tubes nearly 200 m.p.h. Nevertheless, under such conditions of hard work the biggest American locomotives could distribute a couple of tons of hot ash and cinders over the countryside in the even hour, so that high boiler output did not go with high efficiency. This self-regulating feature was one of the principal factors making for the simplicity and success of the steam locomotive.

All the above features were understood and adopted by 1830. After that time only two further fundamental advances were made. First, from 1842, valve motions were adopted that enabled the steam to be cut off in the cylinders at any point, from which point the steam worked by expanding; previously the steam had to be kept on for almost the whole stroke. This led at once to great economy in coal and steam consumption, and to much freer-running locomotives.

The other great advance was high-degree superheating of the steam, introduced at the end of the 19th Century. Ordinary, or saturated, steam at any given pressure has a definite temperature, and each lb. of it occupies a definite number of cubic feet. By adding more heat to the steam after it has passed through the regulator, each lb. was much increased in volume, though the pressure remained the same. Thus each lb. of superheated steam could fill the cylinders more often than a lb. of saturated steam, so there was further economy in coal and water, and again a freer and more lively locomotive.

A third advance, made first in the 1870s, was compounding; that is, after the steam had been used in the first cylinders it was not straightaway exhausted through the chimney, but was led to larger cylinders where it did more work at a lower pressure before it went out through the blast pipe and chimney. This excellent idea never became anything like universal practice, as it did in marine steam engines which worked under much steadier conditions. Power and speed of a locomotive in service are varying all the time from full load to "coasting", that is with steam shut off; and that variation is not so good for efficient compounding.

The friction of the coupled wheels on the rail governed the tractive effort, or pulling power. In general, the maximum tractive effort could not be more than a quarter of the weight on the driving and coupled wheels, otherwise the wheels would slip. So a locomotive that had to draw heavy goods trains needed more adhesion weight, that is weight on the coupled wheels, than a passenger engine, and to obtain this within the permissible axle loads more coupled wheels had to be used. Big goods engines had eight, ten, and even twelve coupled wheels; big passenger engines needed only four or six, and in a few countries eight. This pulling capacity had little to do with horse-power; only a low h.p. is needed to pull a heavy load at low speed along the level. It is speed that brings the need for high power. To pull a medium-weight or heavy train at high speed, or a medium load at a respectable speed up a gradient, needs much h.p., and this means firstly, a boiler capable of generating much steam, and, secondly, cylinders and valves that can use the steam efficiently. Only in the last 25 years of the steam locomotive's 150 years of history did these things really come into vogue—but it was then too late; the electric and diesel systems were coming in.

LOCOMOTIVE WHEEL ARRANGEMENTS

About the end of the 19th Century an American engineer, Whyte, devised a simple system to describe wheel arrangements briefly and clearly. He assumed all engines had leading carrying wheels, driving and coupled wheels, and trailing carrying wheels, which he represented by three numbers, separated by hyphens; where there was no wheel in any group he put 0. Thus an ordinary six-coupled goods engine was 0–6–0; if it had a leading truck it was 2–6–0, and if it had both leading and trailing trucks it was 2–6–2. Engines were assumed to be of tender type; if they were side tanks a T followed the last number, e.g. 0–6–0T; a saddle-tank type was 0–6–0ST, a Great Western type of pannier tank 0–6–0PT, and the old well-type tankers, with tanks low down between the frames, was 0–6–0WT. An articulated locomotive is one with separate groups of wheels in separate frames driven by independent cylinder groups. A Mallet articulated locomotive with three coupled axles in each group would be 0–6–6–0; a Garratt articulated locomotive would be 0–6–0 + 0–6–0.

On the Continent the railways used the number of axles as a base instead of the number of wheels, and without hyphens. A 0–6–0 was 030, and a 4–6–2 was 231. Arising from American habits, certain wheel arrangements also came to have names, which later were used universally. A 4–4–2 was an Atlantic, a 2–6–0 a Mogul, a 4–6–2 a Pacific, a 2–6–2 a Prairie, a 2–8–0 a Consolidation, a 2–8–2 a Mikado, a 4–8–2 a Mountain, and a 2–10–0 a Decapod.

To classify electric and diesel locomotives the axle number system is used, but with letters taking the place of numbers for driving or coupled axles. A is a single driving axle, B two, C three, and so on. To give some indication of the number of motors or method of drive, a small suffix o is added after the letters. Thus a Pacific wheel arrangement is 2–Co–1 if there are three motors, or 2–C–1 if there are one or two large motors with rod drive. A locomotive with two four-wheel bogies is Bo–Bo if there is a motor on each axle, or B–B if there is one motor per bogie driving both axles through gears. Six-wheel bogie notations are Co–Co and C–C; but if the middle axle of such a bogie is motorless the symbol is AIA–AIA. Diesel-hydraulic bogie locomotives always have shafts coupling the axles on a bogie, and so their notations are B–B and C–C.

1802   Trevithick's first locomotive; single cylinder; plain wheels; exhaust up chimney; for a tramroad

1805   Trevithick's Newcastle locomotive: first with flanged wheels, for an edge rail

1812   Blenkinsop; the first commercial locomotive; first rack locomotive; first with two cylinders; first with cranks at right angles; first spring safety valve

1813   First bogie locomotive, Chapman's at Newcastle

1815   Stephenson's second locomotive; the first to have two axles coupled otherwise than by gears

1816   First three-axle locomotive, Stephenson's for Scotland

1825   *Locomotion*, first steam locomotive on a public railway; the first with outside cranks and coupling rods

1826   First four-cylinder locomotive; Wilson's, tried on the Stockton & Darlington Railway

1828   First locomotive on steel springs, Stephenson's six-wheeler on the Stockton & Darlington Railway

1829   Rocket, first multitubular boiler, with blast pipe, cranks at right angles, springs; the first passenger engine

1830   First inside crank axle and two horizontal cylinders, Bury

1830   First smokebox and integral box-form firebox, Stephenson on Liverpool & Manchester Railway

1833   First 0–6–0 inside-cylinder locomotive; first steam brake

1833   First leading bogie fitted to a locomotive, Carmichael, Dundee

1834   Four fixed eccentrics used for first time, Forrester

1840   First long-lap valves with long ($4\frac{1}{2}$ in.) valve travel, Dewrance

1842   First electric locomotive, battery type, Davidson, in Scotland

1842   First application of Stephenson link motion, giving full expansive working

1844   First Walschaerts valve motion, the first of the radial type

1846   First three-cylinder locomotive, Newcastle & Berwick Railway

1851   Continuous expansion locomotive, Eastern Counties Railway

1859   First brick arch and firehole deflector plate, Midland Railway

1859   First injector used in England, L.N.W.R. 2–2–2 engine

1860   First water pick-up troughs, L.N.W.R. in North Wales

1876   First compound locomotive, A. Mallet, in France

1887   First Mallet articulated engine

1897   First high-temperature smoke tube superheater, Schmidt in Germany

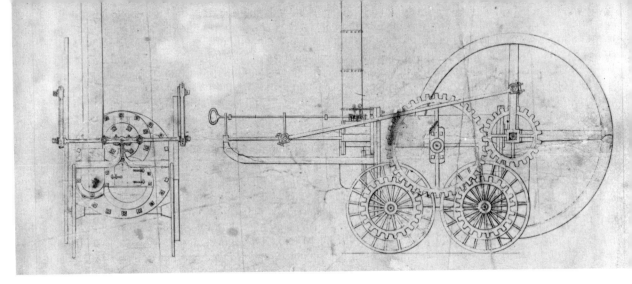

THE FIRST LOCOMOTIVE: Richard Trevithick was the first man to produce rail locomotives. The first, built to his design by Coalbrookdale Ironworks, was completed in 1802; nothing of it is known now except its existence. His second was the famous one that ran at Pen-y-darren Ironworks for some months in 1804. The line was a tramroad, with the rails of cast iron angles, one web of which acted as a flange, the wheels having plain cylindrical treads. The engine was too heavy for such track and was soon laid aside. The single horizontal $8\frac{1}{4}$ in. cylinder had the long stroke of 4 ft. 6 in. and drove the wheels through gears.

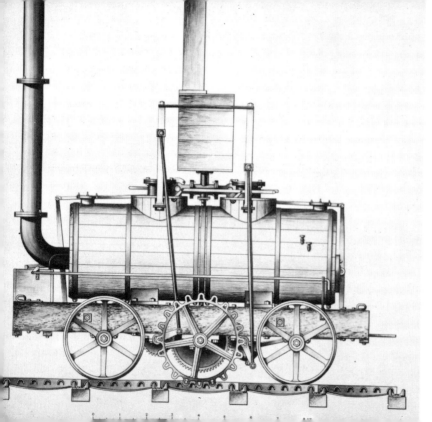

BLENKINSOP'S RACK ENGINES: In 1812 the rack locomotives of Blenkinsop and Murray began working on the Middleton colliery line at Leeds. They were the first commercially successful locomotives anywhere. They had two cylinders immersed in the boiler top with the cranks at right angles, the crank layout being a patent of Murray's in 1802. Each 9 in. by 22 in. cylinder worked on an intermediate shaft geared to a central shaft that carried the rack wheel. The engines looked like six-wheelers, but actually had only four carrying wheels plus one side rack wheel; the last-named engaged with a rack cast on the outside of one of the running rails. Exhaust steam passed not to the chimney but to a *wooden* silencer box and then up a pipe above the boiler top; thus there was no blast pipe.

PUFFING BILLY: After Blenkinsop's first rack locomotives William Hedley at Wylam-on-Tyne made experiments to show that plain wheels were sufficient. Like Pen-y-darren, the Wylam line was a tramroad with thin cast-iron flanged rails. Hedley's first engine started work early in 1814, four or five months before George Stephenson's first, but it had only a single cylinder. The next two had two cylinders; these were *Puffing Billy* now in South Kensington Museum, and *Wylam Dilly* now in Edinburgh Museum. These were built in 1814—15 as four wheelers, but they broke so many rails that they were rebuilt as eight-wheelers to spread the weight. All four axles were driven by gears. Around 1830 they were rebuilt back into four-wheelers

THE KILLINGWORTH ENGINES: George Stephenson built four locomotives at Killingworth over the years 1814—16. All had four plain flanged wheels without rack assistance; all had vertical cylinders let into the boiler top, and connecting rods with cranks at right angles. All had the exhaust steam taken up a pipe in the chimney. First was the *Blucher* with gear drive, in July 1814. Early in 1815 came the second, on a patent of Stephenson & Dodds that covered both crankpin-and-coupling-rod and chain connection of the wheels; which of the two was used is not certain. The third, in the Spring of 1815, was like No. 2. The fourth had Losh & Stephenson patent steam springs. *Blucher* was probably the 14th locomotive built in England.

14

LOCOMOTION: The first steam locomotive to run on a public railway, the first to have outside coupling rods, the first to have lap and lead. Apart from the wheels, the engine preserved at Darlington station is very like it was in the beginning, yet probably not one part—big or small—is the original of 1825.

DATA: *Railway* Stockton & Darlington; *Wheel arrangement* 0–4–0; *Type or class* No.1; *Builder* Robt. Stephenson & Co.; *Year built* 1825; *Cyl. (no.) bore and stroke* (2) 9 in. × 24 in. originally (now 10 in.); *Driving wheel diameter* 4 ft.; *Boiler pressure* 25 lb.; *Tractive effort at 75% pressure* 1,000 lb.; *Total evap. surface* 60 sq. ft.; *Grate area* 4 sq. ft.; *Superheating surface* Nil; *Boiler diameter* 4 ft.; *Coupled wheelbase* 5 ft. 2½ in.; *Engine wheelbase* 5 ft. 2½ in.; *Maximum axle load* 3.35 tons; *Adhesion weight* 6.5 tons; *Total engine weight* 6.5 tons; *Water capacity* 240 gal. (present tender); *Coal capacity* 10 cwt.; *Total wheelbase* 17 ft. 6 in.; *Total length over buffers* 24 ft.; *Engine and tender weight* 9 tons.

THE ROCKET: The *Rocket* of 1829 was the first engine to have the multitubular boiler combined with the blast pipe, which gave automatic regulation of steam production and a much greater rate of evaporation. It had two cylinders with cranks at right angles, and was carried on springs. In these senses it was a forerunner of 99 per cent of all steam locomotives subsequently built, and so was a historic engine technically—quite apart from winning the £500 prize in the Rainhill contest organized by the Liverpool & Manchester Railway. It was really the first passenger locomotive. The barrel, 3 ft. 4 in. dia. and 6 ft. long, contained 25 copper tubes of 3 in. dia. Cylinders were 8 in. by $16\frac{1}{2}$ in. and the driving wheels 4 ft. $8\frac{1}{2}$ in. Weight was $4\frac{1}{2}$ tons.

16

THE PLANET TYPE: With two inside cylinders below the smokebox, a crank axle, and a good frame running from end to end, this was the first great advance on the *Rocket*. It retained the multi-tubular boiler and blast pipe. A four-coupled version was known as the *Samson*.

DATA: *Railway* Liverpool & Manchester; *Wheel arrangement* 2–2–0; *Type or class* Planet; *Builder* Robt. Stephenson & Co.; *Years built* 1830–34; *Cyl. (no.) bore and stroke* (2) 11 in. × 16 in.; *Driving wheel diameter* 5 ft.; *Boiler pressure* 50 lb.; *Tractive effort at 75% pressure* 1,200 lb.; *Total evap. surface* 407 sq. ft.; *Grate area* 5.3 sq. ft.; *Superheating surface* Nil; *Boiler diameter* 3 ft.; *Coupled wheelbase* Nil; *Engine wheelbase* 5ft. 2 in.; *Maximum axle load* 5 tons; *Adhesion weight* 5 tons; *Total engine weight* 8 tons; *Water capacity* approx. 250 gal.; *Coal capacity* approx. $\frac{1}{2}$ ton of coke; *Total wheelbase* 16 ft.; *Total length over buffers* 23 ft. 6 in.; *Engine and tender weight* 11.5 tons.

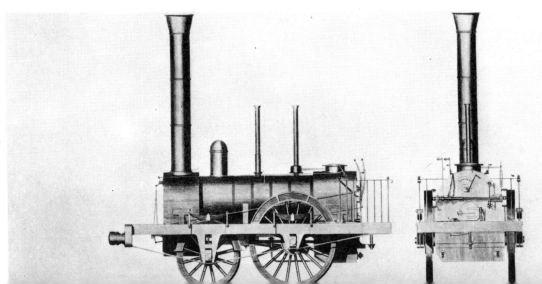

THE BURY'S: Until the last five years or so of his business life, Edward Bury built only 2—2—0 and 0—4—0 engines of small size weighing under 20 tons. Their main features were a bar frame (all other English engines had plate or sandwich frames); two horizontal inside cylinders; and a hemispherical or ''haycock'' firebox.

DATA: *Railway* London & Birmingham; *Wheel arrangement* 2—2—0; *Type or class* Bury; *Builder* Bury, Curtis & Kennedy; *Years built* 1838—40; *Cyl. (no.) bore and stroke* (2) 12 in. × 18 in.; *Driving wheel diameter* 5 ft. 6 in.; *Boiler pressure* 60 lb.; *Tractive effort at 75% pressure* 1,780 lb.; *Total evap. surface* 387 sq. ft.; *Grate area* 6.0 sq. ft.; *Superheating surface* Nil; *Boiler diameter* 4 ft. 2 in.; *Coupled wheelbase* Nil; *Engine wheelbase* 5 ft. 6 in.; *Maximum axle load* 6 tons; *Adhesion weight* 6 tons; *Total engine weight* 10.5 tons; *Water capacity* 500 gal.; *Coal capacity* ¾ ton of coke; *Total wheelbase* 19 ft. 6 in.; *Total length over buffers* 26 ft. 9 in.; *Engine and tender weight* 16.5 tons.

THE NORRIS ENGINES: After Robt. Stephenson & Co., no builder had greater influence on European locomotive practice than Wm. Norris, of Philadelphia, up to 1844–45. He built mainly 4–2–0 types. In England the only examples were on the Birmingham & Gloucester Railway, which had the Lickey incline at 1 in 37.

DATA: *Railway* Birmingham & Gloucester; Austrian; etc.; *Wheel arrangement* 4–2–0; *Type or class* Norris; *Builder* Norris of Philadelphia; *Years built* 1836–43; *Cyl. (no.) bore and stroke* (2) 9.5 in. × 16 in. to 12½ in. × 20 in.; *Driving wheel diameter* 4 ft.; *Boiler pressure* 60 to 80 lb; *Tractive effort at 75% pressure* 1,850 lb. (average); *Total evap. surface* 242 to 504 sq. ft.; *Grate area* 6.4 to 9.5 sq. ft.; *Superheating surface* Nil; *Boiler diameter* 2 ft. 9 in. to 3 ft. 6 in.; *Coupled wheelbase* Nil; *Engine wheelbase* 9 ft. to 9 ft. 6 in.; *Maximum axle load* 4 tons to 9 tons; *Adhesion weight* 4 tons to 9 tons; *Total engine weight* 7¼ tons to 13½ tons; *Water capacity* approx. 450–500 gal.; *Coal capacity* ¾ to 1 ton of coke; *Total wheelbase* 20 ft. 6 in. to 23 ft. 6 in.; *Total length over buffers* 25 ft. to 28 ft.

THE CREWE-ALLAN TYPES: The outside-cylinder 2—2—2 and 2—4—0 classes with inside bearings for the driving and coupled axles, and outside frames and outside bearings for the carrying axles, were evolved by the old Grand Junction Railway to eliminate crank axle fractures, and were perpetuated on the L.N.W.R. until 1857.

DATA: *Railway* London & North Western; *Wheel arrangement* 2—2—2 (and 2—4—0); *Type or class* Crewe passenger (goods); *Builder* Railway, at Crewe; *Years built* 1843–57; *Cyl (no.) bore and stroke* (2) 15¼ in. × 20 in.; *Driving wheel diameter* 6 ft.; *Boiler pressure* 110 lb.; *Tractive effort at 75% pressure* 5,300 lb.; *Total evap. surface* 775 sq. ft.; *Grate area* 10.4 sq. ft.; *Superheating surface* Nil; *Boiler diameter* 3 ft. 6 in.; *Coupled wheelbase* Nil; *Engine wheelbase* 13 ft. 6 in.; *Maximum axle load* 8 tons; *Adhesion weight* 8 tons; *Total engine weight* 19 tons; *Water capacity* 800 gal.; *Coal capacity* 1½ tons; *Total wheelbase* 28 ft.; *Total length over buffers* 37 ft; *Engine and tender weight* 28 tons.

JENNY LIND: Built by E. B. Wilson at Leeds, these engines were considered to be so good looking that the first one was named after the great Swedish singer, then in England. The boiler pressure was 20 per cent higher than that of contemporary engines.

DATA: *Railway* Various English; *Wheel arrangement* 2–2–2; *Type or class* Jenny Lind; *Builder* E. B. Wilson; *Years built* 1847–55; *Cyl. (no.) bore and stroke* (2) 15 in. × 20 in.; *Driving wheel diameter* 6 ft.; *Boiler pressure* 120 lb.; *Tractive effort at 75% pressure* 6,250 lb.; *Total evap. surface* 783 sq. ft.; *Grate area* 12.2 sq. ft.; *Superheating surface* Nil; *Boiler diameter* 3 ft. 8 in.; *Coupled wheelbase* Nil; *Engine wheelbase* 13 ft. 6 in.; *Maximum axle load* 8.7 tons; *Adhesion weight* 8.7 tons; *Total engine weight* 24.1 tons; *Water capacity* approx. 1,250 gal.; *Coal capacity* approx. 1.5/1.75 tons coke; *Total wheelbase* 31 ft. 6 in. approx.; *Total length over buffers* 41 ft. 9 in. approx.; *Engine and tender weight* 39.75 tons.

BROAD-GAUGE "SINGLES": These were the celebrated broad-gauge (7 ft.) singles, with a reputation for high-speed running, much of it very vague as to details. Some lasted almost unaltered until the abolition of the broad gauge in 1892, but by then were of antiquated appearance. They were to the design of Sir Daniel Gooch.
DATA: *Railway* Great Western; *Wheel arrangement* 2–2–2–2; *Type or class* Iron Duke; *Builder* Railway, at Swindon; Rothwell; *Years built* 1847–51; 1854–55; *Cyl. (no.) bore and stroke* (2) 18 in. × 24 in.; *Driving wheel diameter* 8 ft.; *Boiler pressure* 100 lb.; *Tractive effort at 75% pressure* 6,100 lb.; *Total evap. surface* 1,945 sq. ft.; *Grate area* 21.6 sq. ft.; *Superheating surface* Nil; *Boiler diameter* 4 ft. 9¾ in.; *Coupled wheelbase* Nil; *Engine wheelbase* 18 ft. 6 in.; *Maximum axle load* 12.3/14 tons; *Adhesion weight* 12.3/14 tons; *Total engine weight* 35.5/38.2 tons; *Water capacity* 1,760 gal.; *Coal capacity* 1.5 tons (coke); *Total wheelbase* 37 ft. 6 in.; *Total length over buffers* 46 ft. 4 in.; *Engine and tender weight* 52.7 tons.

THE CRAMPTONS: T. R. Crampton believed in putting large single driving wheels behind the firebox and pitching the boiler very low, to get low centre of gravity, sufficient adhesion weight, and a big boiler. The front of the engine was carried on four or six wheels. Largest of them was the *Liverpool*.

DATA: *Railway* L.N.W.R.; *Wheel arrangement* 2—2—2—2—0; *Type or class* Liverpool; *Builder* Bury, Curtis & Kennedy; *Year built* 1848; *Cyl. (no.) bore and stroke* (2) 18 in. × 24 in.; *Driving wheel diameter* 8 ft.; *Boiler pressure* 120 lb.; *Tractive effort at 75% pressure* 7,300 lb.; *Total evap. surface* 2,290 sq. ft.; *Grate area* 21.6 sq. ft.; *Superheating surface* Nil; *Boiler diameter* 5 ft. × 4 ft. 4 in. oval; *Coupled wheelbase* Nil; *Engine wheelbase* 18ft. 6 in.; *Maximum axle load* 12.5 tons; *Adhesion weight* 12.5 tons; *Total engine weight* 35.5 tons; *Water Capacity* 1.5 tons coke; *Total wheelbase* 32 ft. 8 in.; *Total length over buffers* 40 ft. 6 in.; *Engine and tender weight* 55.5 tons.

BRISTOL & EXETER "NINE-FOOTERS": The first batch had 9 ft. driving wheels, the largest ever seen in a non-geared engine in England. The second batch, of which dimensions are given here, had the diameter reduced by 2 in. These engines took over the Great Western Plymouth expresses at Bristol until 1876, when the G.W. bought the B. & E. Railway.
DATA: *Railway* Bristol & Exeter; *Wheel arrangement* 4–2–4T; *Type or class* 1868 construction; *Builder* Rothwell, of Bolton; *Years built* 1853–54; 1868; *Cyl. (no.) bore and stroke* (2) 18 in. × 24 in.; *Driving wheel diameter* 8 ft. 10 in.; *Boiler pressure* 120 lb.; *Tractive effort at 75% pressure* 6,500 lb.; *Total evap. surface* 1,235 sq. ft.; *Grate area* 23 sq. ft.; *Superheating surface* Nil; *Boiler diameter* 4 ft. 3 in.; *Coupled wheelbase* Nil; *Engine wheelbase* 25 ft. 6 in.; *Maximum axle load* 18.5 tons; *Adhesion weight* 18.5 tons; *Total engine weight* 49.75 tons; *Water capacity* 1,430 gal.; *Coal capacity* 1.5 tons; *Total length over buffers* 33 ft. 9 in.

RAMSBOTTOM DX GOODS: This was the first class in England to be built in large numbers—series production rather than mass production. 943 were built at Crewe between 1858 and 1874, and 500 of them were later rebuilt into the Special DX class, the last one of which existed until 1930.

DATA: *Railway* L.N.W.R.; *Wheel arrangement* 0–6–0; *Type or class* DX; *Builder* Railway, at Crewe; *Years built* 1858–74; *Cyl. (no.) bore and stroke* (2) 17 in. × 24 in.; *Driving wheel diameter* 5 ft. 1¼ in.; *Boiler pressure* 120 lb.; *Tractive effort at 75% pressure* 10,200 lb.; *Total evap. surface* 1,102 sq. ft.; *Grate area* 14.9 sq. ft.; *Superheating surface* Nil; *Boiler diameter* 3 ft. 10¾ in.; *Coupled wheelbase* 15 ft. 6 in.; *Engine wheelbase* 15 ft. 6 in.; *Maximum axle load* 10 tons; *Adhesion weight* 27 tons; *Total engine weight* 27 tons; *Water capacity* 1,800 gal.; *Coal capacity* 4 tons; *Total wheelbase* 35 ft. 7 in.; *Total length over buffers* 45 ft. 9 in.; *Engine and tender weight* 53 tons.

THE "AMERICAN" TYPE: Lightweight 4–4–0 engines were the great feature of American motive power during the great railroad development period from 1850 to 1880. They were built in all shapes and sizes, and it is not possible to give more than typical dimensions of the 1860 period, and illustrate an engine that remained in service until 1948.

DATA: *Railway* Numerous American; *Wheel arrangement* 4–4–0; *Type or class* American; *Builder* Norris; Baldwin; Mason; Danforth, etc.; *Years built* 1860–1880; *Cyl. (no.) bore and stroke* (2) 17 in. × 22 in.; *Driving wheel diameter* 5 ft. 6 in.; *Boiler pressure* 120 lb.; *Tractive effort at 75% pressure* 8,700 lb.; *Total evap. surface* 975 sq. ft.; *Grate area* 18.5 sq. ft.; *Superheating surface* Nil; *Boiler diameter* 4 ft. 1 in.; *Coupled wheelbase* 7 ft. 3 in.; *Engine wheelbase* 20 ft. 9 in.; *Maximum axle load* 9.5 tons; *Adhesion weight* 18 tons; *Total engine weight* 26 tons; *Water capacity* 1,000 gal.; *Coal capacity* 2 tons (wood or coke); *Total wheelbase* 38 ft. 6 in.; *Total length over buffers* 45 ft.; *Engine and tender weight* 42 tons.

THE "MET" TANKS: For 40 years until electrification in 1903—07 the dense passenger traffic underground of the Metropolitan and Metropolitan District Railways in London was worked by this type of engine, fitted with simple condensing gear. One is preserved in Clapham Museum.

DATA: *Railway* Metropolitan; *Wheel arrangement* 4—4—OT; *Type or class* A; *Builder* Beyer Peacock; *Years built* 1864—86; *Cyl. (no.) bore and stroke* (2) 17 in. × 24 in.; *Driving wheel diameter* 5 ft. 9 in.; *Boiler pressure* 120/130 lb.; *Tractive effort at 75% pressure* 9,050 lb. (at 120 lb.); *Total evap. surface* 1,016/976 sq. ft.; *Grate area* 19/18 sq. ft.; *Superheating surface* Nil; *Boiler diameter* 4 ft.; *Coupled wheelbase* 8 ft. 10 in./8 ft. 1 in.; *Engine wheelbase* 20 ft. 9 in./20 ft.; *Maximum axle load* 16.7/18.7 tons; *Adhesion weight* 31/36.8 tons. *Total engine weight* 42.2/46.75 tons; *Water capacity* 1,000/1,140 gal.; *Coal capacity* 1.0/1.25 tons; *Total wheelbase* —; *Total length over buffers* 31 ft. 7½ in.

STIRLING'S "EIGHT-FOOTERS": Among the most celebrated steam locomotives ever built, the Stirling singles with 8-ft. wheels varied widely in details; at one time not one of the 53 was exactly like any other, so that only typical dimensions can be given here.

DATA: *Railway* Great Northern; *Wheel arrangement* 4—2—2; *Type or class* G; G2; *Builder* Railway, at Doncaster; *Years built* 1870—1893; *Cyl. (no.) bore and stroke* (2) 18 in. × 28 in.; *Driving wheel diameter* 8 ft. 1 in.; *Boiler pressure* 140/160 lb.; *Tractive effort at 75% pressure* 9,850 lb. (at 140 lb.); *Total evap. surface* 1,093 sq. ft.; *Grate area* 17.75 sq. ft.; *Superheating surface* Nil; *Boiler diameter* 4 ft. 0½ in.; *Coupled wheelbase* Nil; *Engine wheelbase* 22 ft. 11 in.; *Maximum axle load* 15 to 17 tons; *Adhesion weight* 15 to 17 tons; *Total engine weight* 38.5 to 45.2 tons; *Water capacity* 2,700/2,900 gal.; *Coal capacity* 3½/5 tons; *Total wheelbase* 43 ft.; *Total length over buffers* 50 ft. 2 in.; *Engine and tender weight* 65 to 78.75 tons.

"LONG-BOILER" GOODS: A "long boiler" engine was one with the firebox entirely behind the rear axle; this, with the short wheelbase, made the engine rough riding, but meant the engines could go round sharp curves on the mineral lines of the old Stockton & Darlington section of the N.E.R. No. 1275 is preserved at York.

DATA: *Railway* North Eastern; *Wheel arrangement* 0-6-0; *Type or class* 1001; *Builder* Hawthorn; *Railway*, at Darlington; *Years built* 1870–75; *Cyl. (no.) bore and stroke* (2) 17 in. × 24 in.; *Driving wheel diameter* 5 ft.; *Boiler pressure* 140 lb.; *Tractive effort at 75% pressure* 12,150 lb.; *Total evap. surface* 1,578 sq. ft.; *Grate area* 13.3 sq. ft.; *Superheating surface* Nil; *Boiler diameter* 4 ft. 3 in.; *Coupled wheelbase* 11 ft. 10 in.; *Engine wheelbase* 11 ft. 10 in.; *Maximum axle load* 14.1 tons; *Adhesion weight* 35.2 tons; *Total engine weight* 35.2 tons; *Water capacity* 1,600 gal.; *Coal capacity* 4 tons; *Total wheelbase* 36 ft. 3 in.; *Total length over buffers* 48 ft. 11 in.; *Engine and tender weight* 57.3 tons.

BRIGHTON "TERRIERS": The tiny "Terrier" tanks became almost the best-known engines in England despite their diminutive size. They were built to run suburban trains on the South London and East London lines, and in their early days each one made 172 station stops in a working day.

DATA: *Railway* L.B.S.C.R.; *Wheel arrangement* 0—6—0T; *Type or class* A; *Builder* Railway, at Brighton; *Years built* 1872—1880; *Cyl. (no.) bore and stroke* (2) 13 in. × 20 in.; *Driving wheel diameter* 4 ft.; *Boiler pressure* 140 lb.; *Tractive effort at 75% pressure* 7,400 lb.; *Total evap. surface* 528 sq. ft.; *Grate area* 10.3 sq. ft.; *Superheating surface* Nil; *Boiler diameter* 3 ft. 6 in.; *Coupled wheelbase* 12 ft.; *Engine wheelbase* 12 ft.; *Maximum axle load* 8.4 tons; *Adhesion weight* 24.85 tons; *Total engine weight* 24.85 tons; *Water capacity* 500 gal.; *Coal capacity* 12 cwt.; *Total wheelbase* —; *Total length over buffers* 26 ft.

FLETCHER'S 2–4–0s: Very ornate in their original colours and brass-work, these successful engines ran the East Coast Anglo-Scottish expresses between York and Edinburgh from 1871 to 1888. One of them is preserved in York Railway Museum.
DATA: *Railway* North Eastern; *Wheel arrangement* 2–4–0; *Type or class* 901; *Builder* Various; *Years built* 1871–82; *Cyl. (no.) bore and stroke* (2) 17 in. × 24 in.; *some* 17½ in.; *Driving wheel diameter* 7 ft.; *Boiler pressure* 140 lb.; *Tractive effort at 75% pressure* 8,700 lb.; *Total evap. surface* 1,097 sq. ft.; *Grate area* 15.2 sq. ft.; *Superheating surface* Nil; *Boiler diameter* 4 ft. 3 in.; *Coupled wheelbase* 8 ft. 4 in.; *Engine wheelbase* 16 ft. 1 in.; *Maximum axle load* 14 tons; *Adhesion weight* 27.8 tons; *Total engine weight* 36.2 tons; *Water capacity* 2,500 gal.; *Coal capacity* 3.5 tons; *Total wheelbase* 37 ft. 1 in.; *Total length over buffers* 48 ft.; *Engine and tender weight* 69.5 tons.

NORTH EASTERN BTP TANKS: This was one of the first tank-engine types to be built in quantity, though with several variations in details. From 1905 many were fitted to work auto-trains, the fore-runner of "push-and-pull". Others were rebuilt into 0—6—OT, some of which lasted into the days of British Railways.

DATA: *Railway* North Eastern; *Wheel arrangement* 0—4—4T; *Type or class* BTP; *Builder* Neilson; Hawthorn; Railway; *Years built* 1874—83; *Cyl. (no.) bore and stroke* (2) 16 in. × 22 in.; 17 in. × 22 in.; *Driving wheel diameter* 5 ft; 5 ft. 6 in.; *Boiler pressure* 140 lb.; *Tractive effort at 75% pressure* 9,900 lb.; *Total evap. surface* 1,075 sq. ft.; 1,087 sq. ft.; *Grate area* 12.75 sq. ft.; 13 sq. ft.; *Superheating surface* Nil; *Boiler diameter* 4 ft. 2 in.; *Coupled wheelbase* 7 ft. 8 in.; *Engine wheelbase* 21 ft. 8 in.; *Maximum axle load* 13.3 tons; *Adhesion weight* 26.2 tons; *Total engine weight* 44.2 tons; *Water capacity* 960 gal.; 1,000 gal.; *Coal capacity* 2 tons; 2.5 tons; *Total wheelbase* —; *Total length over buffers* 33 ft. 6 in.

NORTH WESTERN "CAULIFLOWERS": F. W. Webb, chief mechanical engineer of the L.N.W.R. for 30 years, excelled in cheap, simple and effective two-cylinder engines of 0−6−0 and 2−4−0 types. This 0−6−0 was one of his best. The name "Cauliflower" arose from the supposed resemblance to that vegetable of the L.N.W.R. crest on the splasher.

DATA: *Railway* L.N.W.R.; *Wheel arrangement* 0−6−0; *Type or class* Cauliflower; *Builder* Railway, at Crewe; *Years built* 1880−1902; *Cyl. (no.) bore and stroke* (2) 18 in. × 24 in.; *Driving wheel diameter* 5 ft. $2\frac{1}{2}$ in.; *Boiler pressure* 150 lb. (140 lb. at first); *Tractive effort at 75% pressure* 14,200 lb.; *Total evap. surface* 1,080 sq. ft.; *Grate area* 17.1 sq. ft.; *Superheating surface* Nil; *Boiler diameter* 4 ft. 1 in.; *Coupled wheelbase* 15 ft. 6 in.; *Engine wheelbase* 15 ft. 6 in.; *Maximum axle load* 13 tons (original 12 tons); *Adhesion weight* 36.5 tons (original 33.4 tons); *Total engine weight* 36.5 tons (original 33.4 tons); *Water capacity* 1,800 gal.; *Coal capacity* 4 tons; *Total wheelbase* 36 ft. $8\frac{1}{2}$ in.; *Total length over buffers* 46 ft. 7 in.; *Engine and tender weight* 61.5 tons.

STROUDLEY'S GLADSTONE: Most famous of many classes introduced by Wm. Stroudley. Almost unique in having large-diameter coupled wheels at the leading end. *Gladstone* itself is preserved in York Railway Museum.

DATA: *Railway* L.B.S.C.R.; *Wheel arrangement* 0–4–2; *Type or class* B; *Builder* Railway, at Brighton; *Years built* 1882–90; *Cyl. (no.) bore and stroke* (2) 18¼ in. × 26 in.; *Driving wheel diameter* 6 ft. 6 in.; *Boiler pressure* 140 lb.; *Tractive effort at 75% pressure* 11,670 lb.; *Total evap. surface* 1,485 sq. ft.; *Grate area* 20.6 sq. ft.; *Superheating surface* Nil; *Boiler diameter* 4 ft. 4 in.; *Coupled wheelbase* 7 ft. 7 in.; *Engine wheelbase* 15 ft. 7 in.; *Maximum axle load* 14.5 tons; *Adhesion weight* 28.3 tons; *Total engine weight* 38.7 tons; *Water capacity* 2,250 gal.; *Coal capacity* 2 tons; *Total wheelbase* 38 ft. 3 in.; *Total length over buffers* 51 ft. 2 in.; *Engine and tender weight* 66.1 tons.

WEBB'S COMPOUND: This was the first three-cylinder compound class (as distinct from odd engines) built by Webb at Crewe. The driving wheels were uncoupled, and if the cylinders were not working in synchronism the wheels could sometimes be seen turning in opposite directions, while the engine remained stationary.

DATA: *Railway* L.N.W R.; *Wheel arrangement* 2-2-2-0.; *Type or class* Compound; *Builder* Railway, at Crewe; *Years built* 1883–84; *Cyl. (no.) bore and stroke* (2) 13 in. × 24 ins. h.p. (1) 26 in. × 24 in. l.p.; *Driving wheel diameter* 6 ft. 7½ in.; *Boiler pressure* 150 lb.; *Tractive effort at 75% pressure* 6,000 lb.; *Total evap. surface* 1,083 sq. ft.; *Grate area* 17.1 sq. ft.; *Superheating surface* Nil; *Boiler diameter* 4 ft. 1 in.; *Coupled wheelbase* 8 ft. 3 in. (rigid, but not coupled); *Engine wheelbase* 17 ft. 7 in.; *Maximum axle load* 14.25 tons; *Adhesion weight* 27.35 tons; *Total engine weight* 37.75 tons; *Water capacity* 1,800 gal.; *Coal capacity* 4 tons; *Total wheelbase* 38 ft. 9 in.; *Total length over buffers* 48 ft. 9 in.; *Engine and tender weight* 63 tons.

CALEDONIAN SINGLE NO. 123: This engine, the last single-driver to work regularly on a British railway, was shown at the Edinburgh Exhibition of 1886, and was a "one-off job". When two years old it was used on some of the Edinburgh "race" trains in 1888. Now preserved in Scotland.

DATA: *Railway* Caledonian; *Wheel arrangement* 4—2—2; *Type or class* 123; *Builder* Neilson; *Year built* 1886; *Cyl. (no.) bore and stroke* (2) 18 in. × 26 in.; *Driving wheel diameter* 7 ft.; *Boiler pressure* 150 lb.; *Tractive effort at 75% pressure* 11,300 lb.; *Total evap. surface* 1,085 sq. ft.; *Grate area* 17.5 sq. ft.; *Superheating surface* Nil; *Boiler diameter* 4 ft. 3 in.; *Coupled wheelbase* Nil; *Engine wheelbase* 21 ft. 1 in.; *Maximum axle load* 17 tons; *Adhesion weight* 17 tons; *Total engine weight* 41.9 tons; *Water capacity* 2,850 gal.; *Coal capacity* 4½ tons; *Total wheelbase* 42 ft. 5½ in.; *Total length over buffers* 51 ft. 9 in.; *Engine and tender weight* 75.4 tons.

WEBB'S "PRECEDENT" CLASS: The simple six-wheel engines bore the brunt of the West Coast passenger traffic from 1885 to 1904 as the bigger and newer Webb compounds were too temperamental to be trusted alone. In the 1895 "Race" *Hardwicke* averaged 67.2 m.p.h. from Crewe to Carlisle.

DATA: *Railway* L.N.W.R.; *Wheel arrangement* 2—4—0; *Type or class* Precedent; *Builder* Railway, at Crewe; *Years built* 1892—96; *Cyl. (no.) bore and stroke* (2) 17 in. × 24 in.; *Driving wheel diameter* 6 ft. 9 in.; *Boiler pressure* 150 lb.; *Tractive effort at 75% pressure* 9,900 lb.; *Total evap. surface* 1,080 sq. ft.; *Grate area* 17 sq. ft.; *Superheating surface* Nil; *Boiler diameter* 4 ft. 1 in.; *Coupled wheelbase* 8 ft. 3 in.; *Engine wheelbase* 15 ft. 8 in.; *Maximum axle load* 12.5 tons; *Adhesion weight* 25 tons; *Total engine weight* 35.6 tons; *Water capacity* 1,800 gal.; *Coal capacity* 4 tons; *Total wheelbase* 36 ft. 10½ in.; *Total length over buffers* 46 ft. 6 in.; *Engine and tender weight* 60 tons.

ADAMS 7-FT. COUPLED, L.S.W.R.: *Comparatively few British 4—4—0 engines had outside cylinders, but the L.S.W.R. had several classes with 6 ft. 7 in. and 7 ft. 1 in. wheels, of graceful outline, and designed by Wm. Adams. Most had the long bogie wheelbase of 7 ft. which helped the appearance.*

DATA: *Railway* L.S.W.R.; *Wheel arrangement* 4—4—0; *Type or class* 577; *Builder* Robt. Stephenson & Co; *Railway; Years built* 1887—93; *Cyl. (no.) bore and stroke* (2) 19 in. × 26 in.; *Driving wheel diameter* 7 ft. 1 in.; *Boiler pressure* 175 lb.; *Tractive effort at 75% pressure* 9,900 lb.; *Total evap. surface* 1,080 sq. ft.; *Grate area* 17 sq. ft.; *Superheating surface* Nil; *Boiler diameter* 4 ft. 1 in.; *Coupled wheelbase* 8 ft. 3 in.; *Engine wheelbase* 15 ft. 8 in.; *Maximum axle load* 12.5 tons; *Adhesion weight* 25 tons; *Total engine weight* 35.6 tons; *Water capacity* 1,800 gal.; *Coal capacity* 4 tons; *Total wheelbase* 44 ft. 3 in.; *Total length over buffers* 53 ft. 8½ in.; *Engine and tender weight* 79 tons.

THE JONES GOODS, HIGHLAND RAILWAY: These 15 engines were the first 4–6–0s to run in Britain, and though mainly for goods traffic they created a minor furore in the railway world. One of them is still preserved in Scotland, unfortunately painted in a colour it never had in service.

DATA: *Railway* Highland; *Wheel arrangement* 4–6–0; *Type or class* Big Goods; *Builder* Sharp Stewart; *Year built* 1894; *Cyl. (no.) bore and stroke* (2) 20 in. × 26 in.; *Driving wheel diameter* 5 ft. 3 in.; *Boiler pressure* 175 lb.; *Tractive effort at 75% pressure* 21,750 lb.; *Total evap. surface* 1,672 sq. ft.; *Grate area* 22.6 sq. ft.; *Superheating surface* Nil; *Boiler diameter* 4 ft. 8 in.; *Coupled wheelbase* 13 ft. 3 in.; *Engine wheelbase* 25 ft.; *Maximum axle load* 14.5 tons; *Adhesion weight* 42 tons; *Total engine weight* 56 tons; *Water capacity* 3,000 gal.; *Coal capacity* 5 tons; *Total wheelbase* 48 ft. 5½ in.; *Total length over buffers* 58 ft. 4½ in.; *Engine and tender weight* 94.35 tons.

GREAT WESTERN 7 ft. 8 in. SINGLES: Considered by many as among the most handsome locomotives built, these 7 ft. 8 in. singles did not have a long life because train weights increased substantially soon after they were built by the wider use of corridor stock and dining cars. In their short life they were speedy and successful.

DATA: *Railway* Great Western Railway; *Wheel arrangement* 4–2–2; *Type or class* 3031; *Builder* Railway, at Swindon; *Years built* 1894–97; *Cyl. (no.) bore and stroke* (2) 19 in. × 24 in.; *Driving wheel diameter* 7 ft. 8½ in.; *Boiler pressure* 160 lb.; *Tractive effort at 75% pressure* 11,200 lb.; *Total evap. surface* 1,467 sq. ft.; *Grate area* 20.8 sq. ft.; *Superheating surface* Nil; *Boiler diameter* 4 ft. 3 in.; *Coupled wheelbase* Nil; *Engine wheelbase* 23 ft. 6 in.; *Maximum axle load* 18.1 tons; *Adhesion weight* 18.1 tons; *Total engine weight* 49 tons; *Water capacity* 3,000 gal.; *Coal capacity* 4 tons; *Total wheelbase* 47 ft. 6¼ in.; *Total length over buffers* 57 ft. 7¾ in.; *Engine and tender weight* 84.5 tons.

THE CALEY "DUNALASTAIRS": These engines in 1896 set the fashion in Britain for large boilers, though the barrel diameter was only 4 ft. 9 in. They had both speed and power, for boilers, cylinders and valves all were excellent. They maintained 55–57 m.p.h. bookings from Carlisle to Perth. The later superheater version shown here began in 1910.

DATA: *Railway* Caledonian; *Wheel arrangement* 4–4–0; *Type or class* 721; *Builder* Railway, at St. Rollox; *Year built* 1896; *Cyl. (no.) bore and stroke* (2) 18¼ in. × 26 in.; *Driving wheel diameter* 6 ft. 6 in.; *Boiler pressure* 160 lb.; *Tractive effort at 75% pressure* 13,300 lb.; *Total evap. surface* 1,403 sq. ft.; *Grate area* 20.6 sq. ft.; *Superheating surface* Nil; *Boiler diameter* 4 ft. 9¼ in.; *Coupled wheelbase* 9 ft.; *Engine wheelbase* 22 ft. 2 in.; *Maximum axle load* 16 tons; *Adhesion weight* 31.25 tons; *Total engine weight* 47 tons; *Water capacity* 3,570 gal.; *Coal capacity* 4.5 tons; *Total wheelbase* 44 ft. 3 in.; *Total length over buffers* 53 ft. 4 in.; *Engine and tender weight* 86 tons.

FIRST ENGLISH ATLANTICS: The first Atlantic, or 4—4—2, engines in England, preceding those of the Lancashire & Yorkshire Railway by only two or three months. The first one, No. 990, is preserved in York Railway Museum.
DATA: *Railway* Great Northern; *Wheel arrangement* 4—4—2; *Type or class* 990; *Builder* Railway, at Doncaster; *Year built* 1898; *Cyl. (no.) bore and stroke* (2) 18¾ in. × 24 in.; *Driving wheel diameter* 6 ft. 7½ in.; *Boiler pressure* 175 lb.; *Tractive effort at 75% pressure* 14,300 lb.; *Total evap. surface* 1,442 sq. ft.; *Grate area* 26.75 sq. ft.; *Superheating surface* Nil; *Boiler diameter* 4 ft. 8 in.; *Coupled wheelbase* 6 ft. 10 in.; *Engine wheelbase* 26 ft. 4 in.; *Maximum axle load* 16 tons; *Adhesion weight* 31 tons; *Total engine weight* 58 tons; *Water capacity* 3,670 gal.; *Coal capacity* 5 tons; *Total wheelbase* 47 ft. 5¼ in.; *Total length over buffers* 56 ft. 10 in.; *Engine and tender weight* 103.1 tons.

THE "LANKY" TANKS: This numerous class at one time worked over half of all the L.Y.R. passenger traffic, and was the only 2—4—2T type in England to work express trains. Later ones were built with superheaters and larger cylinders, and weighed 66 tons.

DATA: *Railway* Lancashire & Yorkshire; *Wheel arrangement* 2—4—2T; *Type or class* 1300; *Builder* Railway, at Horwich; *Years built* 1889—1909; *Cyl. (no.) bore and stroke* (2) 18 in. × 26 in.; *Tractive effort at 75% pressure* 14,850 lb.; *Driving wheel diameter* 5 ft. 8 in.; *Boiler pressure* 160 lb.; *Total evap. surface* 1,216 sq. ft. (1,109 in early engines); *Grate area* 18.75 sq. ft.; *Superheating surface* Nil; *Boiler diameter* 4 ft. 6 in. (4ft. 2 in.); *Coupled wheelbase* 8 ft. 7 in.; *Engine wheelbase* 24 ft. 4 in.; *Maximum axle load* 17.5 tons (16.6); *Adhesion weight* 34.75 tons (31.7); *Total engine weight* 59.2 tons (56); *Water capacity* 1,540 gal. (1,340); *Coal capacity* 3 tons (2); *Total wheelbase* —; *Total length over buffers* 36 ft. (37 ft. 2 in.).

GREAT EASTERN "CLAUD HAMILTONS": This celebrated type evolved at the end of the Victorian era did incredible work throughout the Edwardian years. It could be, and was, thrashed when working the 12-coach Norfolk Coast Express and the Hook Continental up 1 in 70 and 1 in 100 gradients. Oil was the fuel at the beginning.

DATA: *Railway* Great Eastern; *Wheel arrangement* 4–4–0; *Type or class* Claud Hamilton; *Builder* Railway, at Stratford; *Years built* 1900–02; *Cyl. (no.) bore and stroke* (2) 19 in. × 26 in.; *Driving wheel diameter* 7 ft.; *Boiler pressure* 180 lb.; *Tractive effort at 75% pressure* 15,000 lb.; *Total evap. surface* 1,630 sq. ft.; *Grate area* 21.3 sq. ft.; *Superheating surface* Nil; *Boiler diameter* 4 ft. 9 in.; *Coupled wheelbase* 9 ft.; *Engine wheelbase* 23 ft. 6 in.; *Maximum axle load* 16.75 tons; *Adhesion weight* 33.3 tons; *Total engine weight* 50.45 tons; *Water capacity* 2,790 gal.; *Coal capacity* 715 gal. oil + 1½ tons coal; *Total wheelbase* 43 ft. 8 in.; *Total length over buffers* 53 ft.; *Engine and tender weight* 85.5 tons.

N.E.R. EIGHT-COUPLED MINERAL ENGINES: This was the second English 0–8–0 design to be built in numbers, and was an immediate success. Later it was developed into a bigger two-cylinder type (T2), and in 1919 into a three-cylinder version (T3). They handled much of the mineral traffic in north-east England.

DATA: *Railway* North Eastern; *Wheel arrangement* 0–8–0; *Type or class* T and T1; *Builder* Railway, at Gateshead and Darlington; *Years built* 1901–11; *Cyl. (no.) bore and stroke* (2) 20 in. × 26 in.; *Driving wheel diameter* 4 ft. 7¼ in.; *Boiler pressure* 175 lb.; *Tractive effort at 75% pressure* 24,750 lb.; *Total evap. surface* 1,675 sq. ft.; *Grate area* 21.5 sq. ft.; *Superheating surface* Nil; *Boiler diameter* 4 ft. 9 in.; *Coupled wheelbase* 17 ft. 2 in.; *Engine wheelbase* 17 ft. 2 in.; *Maximum axle load* 15.5 tons; *Adhesion weight* 58.3 tons; *Total engine weight* 58.3 tons; *Water capacity* 3,700 gal.; *Coal capacity* 5 tons; *Total wheelbase* 41 ft. 11⅞ in.; *Total length over buffers* 58 ft. 1 in.; *Engine and tender weight* 96.9 tons.

GREAT WESTERN "CITIES": *City of Truro* is preserved at Swindon museum on the basis of being the first British engine to exceed 100 m.p.h.; but alas, is open to doubt as the records are far too vague for any claim to be substantiated. But the Cities were good and speedy engines.

DATA: *Railway* Great Western; *Wheel arrangement* 4–4–0; *Type or class* City; *Builder* Railway, at Swindon; *Year built* 1903; *Cyl. (no.) bore and stroke* (2) 18 in. × 26 in.; *Driving wheel diameter* 6 ft. 8½ in.; *Boiler pressure* 195 lb.; *Tractive effort at 75% pressure* 15,340 lb.; *Total evap. surface* 1,818 sq. ft.; *Grate area* 20.6 sq. ft.; *Superheating surface* Nil; *Boiler diameter* 5 ft. 6 in./4 ft. 10¾ in. taper; *Coupled wheelbase* 8 ft. 6 in.; *Engine wheelbase* 22 ft. 6 in.; *Maximum axle load* 18.5 tons; *Adhesion weight* 36 tons; *Total engine weight* 55.5 tons; *Water capacity* 3,000 gal.; *Coal capacity* 4 tons; *Total wheelbase* 46 ft. 9¼ in.; *Total length over buffers* 56 ft. 4¾ in.; *Engine and tender weight* 92.25 tons.

THE BIG-BOILERED ATLANTICS: The large-boilered Ivatt Atlantics were the first engines built in England with a wide firebox, though not the first of such to run in England, or even on the G.N.R. After superheating and the fitting of bigger cylinders they did marvellous work.

DATA: *Railway* Great Northern; *Wheel arrangement* 4—4—2; *Type or class* 251; *Builder* Railway, at Doncaster; *Year built* 1904; *Cyl. (no.) bore and stroke* (2) 18.75 in. × 24 in.; *Driving wheel diameter* 6 ft. 7½ in.; *Boiler pressure* 175 lb.; *Tractive effort at 75% pressure* 17,000 lb.; *Total evap. surface* 1,458 sq. ft.; *Grate area* 28.4 sq. ft.; *Superheating surface* Nil; *Boiler diameter* 5 ft. 6 in.; *Coupled wheelbase* 6 ft. 10 in.; *Engine wheelbase* 26 ft. 4 in.; *Maximum axle load* 18.5 tons; *Adhesion weight* 36 tons; *Total engine weight* 65.5 tons; *Water capacity* 3,670 gal.; *Coal capacity* 5 tons; *Total wheelbase* 48 ft. 5½ in.; *Total length over buffers* 57 ft. 10¼ in.; *Engine and tender weight* 106.5 tons.

NORTH EASTERN HEAVY GOODS: The squat 5 ft. 6 in. boiler gave immense steam capacity, though the grate and fire-box were not particularly big. The engines were capable of sustained hard work with few repairs, and were among the last steam locomotives to work in Northumberland and County Durham.

DATA: *Railway* North Eastern; *Wheel arrangement* 0–6–0; *Type or class* P2 & P3; *Builder* Railway, at Darlington; *Years built* 1904–10; *Cyl. (no.) bore and stroke* (2) 18.5 in × 26 in.; *Driving wheel diameter* 4 ft. 7$\frac{1}{4}$ in.; *Boiler pressure* 180 lb. (originally 200 lb.); *Tractive effort at 75% pressure* 21,800 lb.; *Total evap. surface* 1,658 sq. ft.; *Grate area* 20 sq. ft.; *Superheating surface* Nil; *Boiler diameter* 5 ft. 6 in.; *Coupled wheelbase* 16 ft. 6 in.; *Engine wheelbase* 16 ft. 6 in.; *Maximum axle load* 17 tons; *Adhesion weight* 47.7 tons; *Total engine weight* 47.7 tons; *Water capacity* 3,040 gal.; *Coal capacity* 5 tons; *Total wheelbase* 39 ft. 0$\frac{3}{4}$ in.; *Total length over buffers* 52 ft. 2$\frac{1}{4}$ in.; *Engine and tender weight* 82.1 tons.

MIDLAND COMPOUNDS: The first of the Deeley three-cylinder compounds on the old Midland Railway, which 20 years later was developed further into the first standard express passenger engine of the L.M.S.R. Engine No. 1000 is preserved at Clapham.

DATA: *Railway* Midland; *Wheel arrangement* 4–4–0; *Type or class* 1000; *Builder* Railway, at Derby; *Years built* 1905–06; *Cyl. (no.) bore and stroke* (1) 19 in. × 26 in. h.p. (2) 21 in. × 26 in. l.p.; *Driving wheel diameter* 7 ft.; *Boiler pressure* 200 lb.; *Tractive effort at 75% pressure* 17,000 lb.; *Total evap. surface* 1,458 sq. ft.; *Grate area* 28.4 sq. ft.; *Superheating surface* Nil; *Boiler diameter* 4 ft. 8 in.; *Coupled wheelbase* 9 ft. 6 in.; *Engine wheelbase* 24 ft. 4½ in.; *Maximum axle load* 19.75 tons; *Adhesion weight* 39.1 tons; *Total engine weight* 59.8 tons; *Water capacity* 3,500 gal.; *Coal capacity* 7 tons; *Total wheelbase* 48 ft. 3¼ in.; *Total length over buffers* 57 ft. 3½ in.; *Engine and tender weight* 102.65 tons.

CARDEAN: The Cardean-class engines were among the most notable British locomotives of the pre-1914 period—as massive as a warship, capable of good medium-speed performance, but not able to develop anything like the power suggested by the size.

DATA: *Railway* Caledonian; *Wheel arrangement* 4–6–0; *Type or class* 903; *Builder* Railway, at St. Rollox; *Year built* 1906; *Cyl. (no.) bore and stroke* (2) 20 in. × 26 in.; *Driving wheel diameter* 6 ft. 6 in.; *Boiler pressure* 200 lb.; *Tractive effort at 75% pressure* 20,000 lb.; *Total evap. surface* 2,460 sq. ft.; *Grate area* 26 sq. ft.; *Superheating surface* Nil; *Boiler diameter* 5 ft. 2½ in.; *Coupled wheelbase* 15 ft. 0 in.; *Engine wheelbase* 28 ft. 8 in.; *Maximum axle load* 18.7 tons; *Adhesion weight* 54 tons; *Total engine weight* 73 tons; *Water capacity* 5,000 gal.; *Coal capacity* 6 tons; *Total wheelbase* 55 ft. 6 in.; *Total length over buffers* 65 ft. 6 in.; *Engine and tender weight* 130 tons.

GREAT WESTERN "STARS": The first of the long line of Churchward four-cylinder high-pressure engines of 4—6—0 type, outstanding in their power performance in the pre-1914 era, and sterling workers up to the final withdrawals in the 1950s.
DATA: *Railway* Great Western; *Wheel arrangement* 4—6—0; *Type or class* Star; *Builder* Railway, at Swindon; *Years built* 1907–14; *Cyl. (no.) bore and stroke* (4) 14.25 in.; × 26 in.; *Driving wheel diameter* 6 ft. 8½ in.; *Boiler pressure* 225 lb.; *Tractive effort at 75% pressure* 22,200 lb.; *Total evap. surface* 2,143 sq. ft.; *Grate area* 27.1 sq. ft.; *Superheating surface* Nil originally; *Boiler diameter* 5 ft. 6 in./4 ft. 10¾ in. taper; *Coupled wheelbase* 14 ft. 9 in.; *Engine wheelbase* 27 ft. 3 in.; *Maximum axle load* 18.6 tons; *Adhesion weight* 55.4 tons; *Total engine weight* 75.6 tons; *Water capacity* 3,500 gal.; *Coal capacity* 5 tons; *Total wheelbase* 53 ft. 6¼ in.; *Total length over buffers* 64 ft. 1¾ in.; *Engine and tender weight* 115.6 tons.

THE GREAT BEAR: The first English Pacific—an elongated version of the Star-class four-cylinder 4–6–0, and not very successful. Because of the axle loading and long awkward wheelbase it was confined to the London-Bristol route. Rebuilt into a 4–6–0 in 1924.

DATA: *Railway* Great Western; *Wheel arrangement* 4–6–2; *Type or class* 111; *Builder* Railway, at Swindon; *Year built* 1908; *Cyl. (no.) bore and stroke* (4) 15 in. × 26 in.; *Driving wheel diameter* 6 ft. 8½ in.; *Boiler pressure* 225 lb.; *Tractive effort at 75% pressure* 24,600 lb.; *Total evap. surface* 2,856 sq. ft.; *Grate area* 41.8 sq. ft.; *Superheating surface* 545 sq. ft.; *Boiler diameter* 6 ft./5 ft. 6 in. taper; *Coupled wheelbase* 14 ft.; *Engine wheelbase* 34 ft. 6 in.; *Maximum axle load* 20.1 tons; *Adhesion weight* 60.2 tons; *Total engine weight* 97.2 tons; *Water capacity* 3,500 gal.; *Coal capacity* 6 tons; *Total wheelbase* 61 ft. 0½ in.; *Total length over buffers* 71 ft. 2¼ in.; *Engine and tender weight* 142.75 tons.

TILBURY TANKS: Several classes of this wheel arrangement were built for the outer suburban and Southend express trains of "the Tilbury" from 1879 until just before World War 1, size and power increasing gradually. They were among the most successful passenger tank engines to operate in England.

DATA: *Railway* London, Tilbury & Southend; *Wheel arrangement* 4-4-2T; *Type or class* 39-40; *Builder* Sharp Stewart; *Year built* 1897; *Cyl. (no.) bore and stroke* (2) 18 in. × 26 in.; *Driving wheel diameter* 6 ft. 6 in.; *Boiler pressure* 170 lb.; *Tractive effort at 75% pressure* 13,850 lb.; *Total evap. surface* 1,027 sq. ft.; *Grate area* 19.8 sq. ft.; *Superheating surface* Nil; *Boiler diameter* 4 ft. 1 in.; *Coupled wheelbase* 8 ft. 9 in.; *Engine wheelbase* 30 ft. 9½ in.; *Maximum axle load* 17.75 tons; *Adhesion weight* 35.15 tons; *Total engine weight* 63.2 tons; *Water capacity* 1,500 gal.; *Coal capacity* 2.75 tons; *Total wheelbase* —; *Total length over buffers* 39 ft. 6 in.

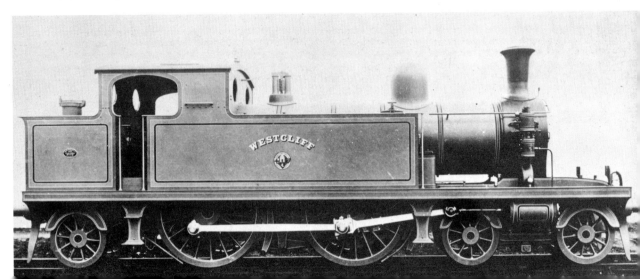

L.N.W.R. GEORGE V: These were the superheated version of the Precursor class introduced in 1904; both types were worked very hard on West Coast and London-Birmingham fast heavy trains until 1925–27, and were among the best engines the North Western ever had.

DATA: *Railway* L.N.W.R.; *Wheel arrangement* 4–4–0; *Type or class* George V; *Builder* Railway, at Crewe; *Year built* 1910; *Cyl. (no.) bore and stroke* (2) 20.5 in. × 26 in.; *Driving wheel diameter* 6 ft. 9 in.; *Boiler pressure* 175 lb.; *Tractive effort at 75% pressure* 17,600 lb.; *Total evap. surface* 1,547 sq. ft.; *Grate area* 22.4 sq. ft.; *Superheating surface* 302 sq. ft.; *Boiler diameter* 5 ft. 3 in.; *Coupled wheelbase* 10 ft.; *Engine wheelbase* 25 ft. 1½ in.; *Maximum axle load* 19.25 tons; *Adhesion weight* 38.25 tons; *Total engine weight* 59.85 tons; *Water capacity* 3,000 gal.; *Coal capacity* 5 tons; *Total wheelbase* 47 ft. 2¾ in.; *Total length over buffers* 56 ft. 6 in.; *Engine and tender weight* 97.85 tons.

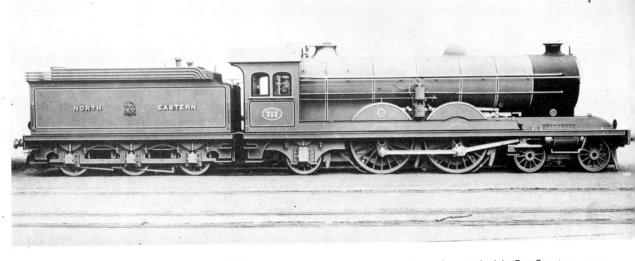

NORTH EASTERN 3-CYLINDER ATLANTICS: These handsome smooth-running engines worked the East Coast expresses from 1911 to 1925. The three cylinders had three sets of Stephenson valve motion, and so in the 3 ft. between the driving axleboxes were crowded one crank throw, one connecting rod, and six eccentrics.

DATA: *Railway* North Eastern; *Wheel arrangement* 4–4–2; *Type or class* Z; *Builder* NBL; Railway, at Darlington; *Years built* 1911–18; *Cyl. (no.) bore and stroke* (3) 16.5 in. × 26 in.; *Driving wheel diameter* 6 ft. 10 in.; *Boiler pressure* 160 lb. (later 175 lb.); *Tractive effort at 75% pressure* 15,500 lb. (later 17,000 lb.); *Total evap. surface* 1,979 sq. ft.; *Grate area* 27 sq. ft.; *Superheating surface* 530 sq. ft.; *Boiler diameter* 5 ft. 6 in.; *Coupled wheelbase* 7 ft. 7 in.; *Engine wheelbase* 29 ft. 6 in.; *Maximum axle load* 20.1 tons (later 20.8 tons); *Adhesion weight* 39.85 tons (later 40.75 tons); *Total engine weight* 77.1 tons (later 79.25 tons); *Water capacity* 4,125 gal.; *Coal capacity* 5½ tons; *Total wheelbase* 53 ft. 3⅛ in.; *Total length over buffers* 64 ft. 1⅜ in.; *Engine and tender weight* 125.85 tons.

THE R.O.D. ENGINES: This design of the G.C.R. was adopted by the Government during World War 1, and 521 were built for the Railway Operating Division, and so all became loosely known as the ROD engines. They were fine reliable engines that could stand illimitable knocking about.

DATA: *Railway* Great Central; *Wheel arrangement* 2–8–0; *Type or class* 8K; *Builder* Railway; and various builders; *Years built* 1911–19; *Cyl. (no.) bore and stroke* (2) 21 in. × 26 in.; *Driving wheel diameter* 4 ft. 8 in.; *Boiler pressure* 180 lb.; *Tractive effort at 75% pressure* 27,650 lb.; *Total evap. surface* 1,691 sq. ft.; *Grate area* 26.2 sq. ft.; *Superheating surface* 318 sq. ft.; *Boiler diameter* 5 ft.; *Coupled wheelbase* 17 ft. 1 in.; *Engine wheelbase* 25 ft. 5 in.; *Maximum axle load* 17.4 tons; *Adhesion weight* 67 tons; *Total engine weight* 73.7 tons; *Water capacity* 4,000 gal.; *Coal capacity* 7 tons; *Total wheelbase* 51 ft. 2½ in.; *Total length over buffers* 61 ft. 9 in.; *Engine and tender weight* 117.5 tons.

GREAT EASTERN 4–6–0s: Because of certain bridges these engines had to be built to light axle load, but they were good steamers and good pullers, and took over the principal G.E.R. trains, getting heavier year by year, from the Claud Hamilton 4–4–0s (see page 44).

DATA: *Railway* Great Eastern; *Wheel arrangement* 4–6–0; *Type or class* S.69; *Builder* Railway, at Stratford; *Years built* 1912–22; *Cyl. (no.) bore and stroke* (2) 20 in. × 28 in.; *Driving wheel diameter* 6 ft. 6 in.; *Boiler pressure* 180 lb.; *Tractive effort at 75% pressure* 19,400 lb.; *Total evap. surface* 1,633 sq. ft.; *Grate area* 26.5 sq. ft.; *Superheating surface* 286 sq. ft.; *Boiler diameter* 5 ft.; *Coupled wheelbase* 14 ft.; *Engine wheelbase* 28 ft. 6 in.; *Maximum axle load* 16.0 tons; *Adhesion weight* 44 tons; *Total engine weight* 64 tons; *Water capacity* 3,700 gal.; *Coal capacity* 4 tons; *Total wheelbase* 48 ft. 3 in.; *Total length over buffers* 57 ft. 7 in.; *Engine and tender weight* 103.25 tons.

NORTH WESTERN 4-CYLINDER CLAUGHTONS: This was really the first and last attempt of the L.N.W.R. at a big passenger engine. Restrictions of weight, and of equipment at Crewe works, limited the size of the boiler, and as cylinder performance was not outstanding they were generally mediocre.

DATA: *Railway* L.N.W.R.; *Wheel arrangement* 4-6-0; *Type or class* Claughton; *Builder* Railway, at Crewe; *Year built* 1913; *Cyl. (no.) bore and stroke* (4) 15¾ in. × 26 in.; *Driving wheel diameter* 6 ft. 9 in.; *Boiler pressure* 175 lb.; *Tractive effort at 75% pressure* 20,900 lb.; *Total evap. surface* 1,818 sq. ft.; *Grate area* 30.5 sq. ft.; *Superheating surface* 413 sq. ft.; *Boiler diameter* 5 ft.; *Coupled wheelbase* 15 ft. 3 in.; *Engine wheelbase* 29 ft.; *Maximum axle load* 19.8 tons; *Adhesion weight* 59 tons; *Total engine weight* 77.75 tons; *Water capacity* 3,000 gal.; *Coal capacity* 6 tons; *Total wheelbase* 54 ft.; *Total length over buffers* 63 ft. 4¾ in.; *Engine and tender weight* 117 tons.

THE LICKEY BANKER: This unusual engine, the only 0–10–0 tender engine to run in England, and known irreverently as "Big Bertha", was used all its life on a stretch of line less than 3 miles long, banking trains up the well-known Lickey incline at 1 in 37 between Bristol and Birmingham.

DATA: *Railway* Midland; *Wheel arrangement* 0–10–0; *Type or class* 2290; *Builder* Railway, at Derby; *Year built* 1920; *Cyl. (no.) bore and stroke* (4) 16¾ in. × 28 in.; *Driving wheel diameter* 4 ft. 7½ in.; *Boiler pressure* 180 lb.; *Tractive effort at 75% pressure* 38,000 lb.; *Total evap. surface* 1,718 sq. ft.; *Grate area* 31.5 sq. ft.; *Superheating surface* 445 sq. ft.; *Boiler diameter* 5 ft. 4 in.; *Coupled wheelbase* 20 ft. 11 in.; *Engine wheelbase* 20 ft. 11 in.; *Maximum axle load* 15.5 tons; *Adhesion weight* 73.6 tons; *Total engine weight* 73.6 tons; *Water capacity* 2,050 gal.; *Coal capacity* 4 tons; *Total wheelbase* 46 ft. 3¾ in.; *Total length over buffers* 61 ft. 0⅝ in.; *Engine and tender weight* 105.1 tons.

G.W. 8-COUPLED MIXED TRAFFIC: The first "big" Great Western mixed-traffic engine, much more powerful than the numerous Moguls, excellent for heavy fast goods trains and excursions; but not being able to operate express passenger trains the class was not multiplied beyond eight engines.

DATA: *Railway* Great Western; *Wheel arrangement* 2–8–0; *Type or class* 4700; *Builder* Railway, at Swindon; *Years built* 1920–22; *Cyl. (no.) bore and stroke* (2) 19 in. × 30 in.; *Driving wheel diameter* 5 ft. 8 in.; *Boiler pressure* 225 lb.; *Tractive effort at 75% pressure* 27,000 lb.; *Total evap. surface* 2,232 sq. ft.; *Grate area* 30.3 sq. ft.; *Superheating surface* 289 sq. ft.; *Boiler diameter* 6 ft. 0 in./5 ft. 6 in. taper; *Coupled wheelbase* 20 ft. 0 in.; *Engine wheelbase* 29 ft. 3 in.; *Maximum axle load* 19.6 tons; *Adhesion weight* 73.4 tons; *Total engine weight* 82 tons; *Water capacity* 4,000 gal.; *Coal capacity* 6 tons; *Total wheelbase* 56 ft. 10½ in.; *Total length over buffers* 66 ft. 4¼ in.; *Engine and tender weight* 128.7 tons.

GREAT NORTHERN BIG-BOILER MOGUL: The 6-ft. boiler of these engines caused a great stir when the first ones came out; and the high steam-raising power, large cylinder capacity, and great adhesion weight brought the mixed-traffic engine in England on to quite a new footing.

DATA: *Railway* Great Northern; *Wheel arrangement* 2–6–0; *Type or class* 1000; *Builder* Railway, at Doncaster; *Years built* 1920 onwards; *Cyl. (no.) bore and stroke* (3) 18$\frac{1}{2}$ in. × 26 in.; *Driving wheel diameter* 5 ft. 8 in.; *Boiler pressure* 180 lb.; *Tractive effort at 75% pressure* 26,500 lb.; *Total evap. surface* 1,901 sq. ft.; *Grate area* 28 sq. ft.; *Superheating surface* 407 sq. ft.; *Boiler diameter* 6 ft.; *Coupled wheelbase* 16 ft. 3 in.; *Engine wheelbase* 25 ft. 2 in.; *Maximum axle load* 20 tons; *Adhesion weight* 60 tons; *Total engine weight* 71.7 tons; *Water capacity* 3,500 gal.; *Coal capacity* 6.5 tons; *Total wheelbase* 48 ft. 2 in.; *Total length over buffers* 57 ft. 7$\frac{1}{2}$ in.; *Engine and tender weight* 114.8 tons.

SOUTH WESTERN HUMP SHUNTER: Built for hump and heavy shunting services in the Feltham yard to the south-west of London, these engines were similar in many respects to some 4—6—2T built at the same time to transfer freight trains north-east from Feltham to Willesden on the L.N.W.R.

DATA: *Railway* L.S.W.R.; *Wheel arrangement* 4—8—0T; *Type or class* G.16; *Builder* Railway, at Eastleigh; *Year built* 1921; *Cyl. (no.) bore and stroke* (2) 22 in. × 28 in.; *Driving wheel diameter* 5 ft. 1 in.; *Boiler pressure* 180 lb.; *Tractive effort at 75% pressure* 30,000 lb.; *Total evap. surface* 1,406 sq. ft.; *Grate area* 27 sq. ft.; *Superheating surface* 252 sq. ft.; *Boiler diameter* 4 ft. 10¾ in.; *Coupled wheelbase* 18 ft.; *Engine wheelbase* 32 ft.; *Maximum axle load* 18.5 tons; *Adhesion weight* 73 tons; *Total engine weight* 95.2 tons; *Water capacity* 2,000 gal.; *Coal capacity* 3.5 tons; *Total wheelbase* —; *Total length over buffers* 42 ft. 10¼ in.

BRIGHTON BALTICS: Before World War I two or three engines of this wheel arrangement had been built for the London to Brighton expresses, then entirely steam worked. The engines described here were a redesign with all the good points in and the bad points out. After electrification got going on the S.R., they were rebuilt as 4–6–0 tender engines.
DATA: *Railway* L.B.S.C.R.; *Wheel arrangement* 4–6–4T; *Type or class* L; *Builder* Railway, at Brighton; *Year built* 1921; *Cyl. (no.) bore and stroke* (2) 22 in. × 28 in.; *Driving wheel diameter* 6 ft. 9 in.; *Boiler pressure* 170 lb.; *Tractive effort at 75% pressure* 22,100 lb.; *Total evap. surface* 1,816 sq. ft.; *Grate area* 26.7 sq. ft.; *Superheating surface* 323 sq. ft.; *Boiler diameter* 5 ft. 4 in.; *Coupled wheelbase* 14 ft. 9 in.; *Engine wheelbase* 40 ft.; *Maximum axle load* 19.2 tons; *Adhesion weight* 56.75 tons; *Total engine weight* 98.5 tons; *Water capacity* 2,685 gal.; *Coal capacity* 3.5 tons; *Total wheelbase* —; *Total length over buffers* 50 ft. 4¾ in.

G.W. PANNIER TANKS: For many years, right up to 1947–48, the G.W.R. built six-coupled pannier tanks for shunting and trip-train working. The panniers—side tanks attached to the boiler and not to the running plates—brought the "P" into the wheel arrangement symbol. British Railways also built one batch, in 1950.

DATA: *Railway* Great Western; *Wheel arrangement* 0–6–0PT; *Type or class* 5700; *Builder* Railway, at Swindon; *Years built* 1928–48; *Cyl. (no.) bore and stroke* (2) 17½ in. × 24 in.; *Driving wheel diameter* 4 ft. 7½ in.; *Boiler pressure* 200 lb.; *Tractive effort at 75% pressure* 19,800 lb.; *Total evap. surface* 1,178 sq. ft.; *Grate area* 15.3 sq. ft.; *Superheating surface* Nil; *Boiler diameter* 4 ft. 5 in.; *Coupled wheelbase* 15 ft. 6 in.; *Engine wheelbase* 15 ft. 6 in.; *Maximum axle load* 16.75 tons; *Adhesion weight* 47.5 tons; *Total engine weight* 47.5 tons; *Water capacity* 1,200 gal.; *Coal capacity* 2 tons; *Total wheelbase* —; *Total length over buffers* 31 ft. 2 in.

FOUR-CYLINDER SUBURBAN TANK: This remarkable engine was built to give high acceleration with the N.S.R. frequent-stop passenger trains; the four cylinders were set with cranks at 135 deg. to get eight exhaust beats per revolution. After grouping in 1923 it was rebuilt into an 0—6—0 tender engine.

DATA: *Railway* North Staffordshire; *Wheel arrangement* 0—6—0T; *Type or class* 23; *Builder* Railway, at Stoke; *Year built* 1922; *Cyl. (no.) bore and stroke* (4) 14 in. × 24 in.; *Driving wheel diameter* 4 ft. 6 in.; *Boiler pressure* 160 lb.; *Tractive effort at 75% pressure* 20,900 lb.; *Total evap. surface* 857 sq. ft.; *Grate area* 17.5 sq. ft.; *Superheating surface* 195 sq. ft.; *Boiler diameter* 4 ft. 7 in.; *Coupled wheelbase* 16 ft. 6 in.; *Engine wheelbase* 16 ft. 6 in.; *Maximum axle load* 19.5 tons; *Adhesion weight* 56.65 tons; *Total engine weight* 56.65 tons; *Water capacity* 900 gal.; *Coal capacity* 2.25 tons; *Total wheelbase* —; *Total length over buffers* 32 ft. 5½ in.; *Engine and tender weight* Nil.

GREAT WESTERN "CASTLES": Probably the most successful express engines the Great Western ever possessed; developed directly from the Stars and with bigger boilers and a slightly higher axle load. Some of the Stars were rebuilt into Castles in the 1920s and 1930s.

DATA: *Railway* Great Western; *Wheel arrangement* 4–6–0; *Type or class* Castle; *Builder* Railway, at Swindon; *Years built* 1923–27; 1932–50; *Cyl. (no.) bore and stroke* (4) 15 in. × 26 in.; *Driving wheel diameter* 6 ft. 8½ in.; *Boiler pressure* 225 lb.; *Tractive effort at 75% pressure* 24,600 lb.; *Total evap. surface* 2,150 sq. ft.; *Grate area* 30.3 sq. ft.; *Superheating surface* 262 sq. ft.; *Boiler diameter* 5 ft. 9 in./5 ft. 2 in. taper; *Coupled wheelbase* 14 ft. 9 in.; *Engine wheelbase* 27 ft. 3 in.; *Maximum axle load* 19.7 tons; *Adhesion weight* 58.85 tons; *Total engine weight* 79.85 tons; *Water capacity* 4,000 gal. (3,500 gal. originally); *Coal capacity* 6 tons; *Total wheelbase* 54 ft. 6½ in.; *Total length over buffers* 65 ft. 2 in.; *Engine and tender weight* 126.55 tons (with larger tender than original).

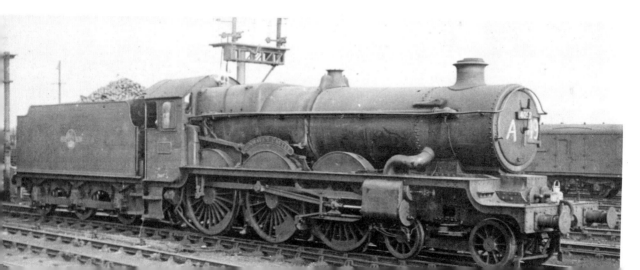

GREAT WESTERN "KINGS": This was the culmination of the four-cylinder 4—6—0 on the G.W.R.—right up to the new weight limits allowed by new rails and bridge strengthening, and allowed only on the London-Plymouth, London-Bristol and London-Wolverhampton routes. 30 engines were built

DATA: *Railway* Great Western; *Wheel arrangement* 4—6—0; *Type or class* King; *Builder* Railway, at Swindon; *Years built* 1927—30; *Cyl. (no.) bore and stroke* (4) 16.25 in. × 28 in.; *Driving wheel diameter* 6 ft. 6 in.; *Boiler pressure* 250 lb.; *Tractive effort at 75% pressure* 35,400 lb.; *Total evap. surface* 2,201 sq. ft.; *Grate area* 34.3 sq. ft.; *Superheating surface* 313 sq. ft.; *Boiler diameter* 6 ft. 0 in./5 ft. 6 in. taper; *Coupled wheelbase* 16 ft. 3 in.; *Engine wheelbase* 29 ft. 3 in.; *Maximum axle load* 22.5 tons; *Adhesion weight* 67.5 tons; *Total engine weight* 89.0 tons; *Water capacity* 4,000 gal.; *Coal capacity* 6 tons; *Total wheelbase* 57 ft. 5½ in.; *Total length over buffers* 68 ft. 2 in.; *Engine and tender weight* 135.7 tons.

FIRST GRESLEY PACIFIC: The first English ''production'' Pacific—the first of which more than one was built, and the first ''Gresley'' Pacific. These engines worked the Anglo-Scottish expresses from 1923 to 1930, when the design was developed into the A3 class.

DATA: *Railway* Great Northern; *Wheel arrangement* 4—6—2; *Type or class* A1 (LNER); *Builder* Railway, at Doncaster; NBL; *Years built* 1922—28; *Cyl. (no.) bore and stroke* (3) 20 in. × 26 in.; *Driving wheel diameter* 6 ft. 8 in.; *Boiler pressure* 180 lb.; *Tractive effort at 75% pressure* 26,350 lb.; *Total evap. surface* 2,930 sq. ft.; *Grate area* 41. 2 sq. ft.; *Superheating surface* 525 sq. ft.; *Boiler diameter* 6 ft. 5 in./5 ft. 9 in. taper; *Coupled wheelbase* 14 ft. 6 in.; *Engine wheelbase* 35 ft. 9 in.; *Maximum axle load* 20 tons; *Adhesion weight* 60 tons; *Total engine weight* 92.45 tons; *Water capacity* 5,000 gal.; *Coal capacity* 8 tons; *Total wheelbase* 60 ft. 10⅝ in.; *Total length over buffers* 70 ft. 5 in.; *Engine and tender weight* 148.75 tons.

L.N.E.R. STREAMLINED PACIFICS: These were the greatest Gresley Pacifics, and day after day touched 100 m.p.h. on the Silver Jubilee and Coronation streamlined trains. One of them, *Mallard*, preserved in Clapham Museum, holds the world record of 125 m.p.h. for a steam locomotive.

DATA: *Railway* London & North Eastern; *Wheel arrangement* 4–6–2; *Type or class* A4; *Builder* Railway, at Doncaster; *Years built* 1935–38; *Cyl. (no.) bore and stroke* (3) $18\frac{1}{2}$ in. $\times$ 26 in.; *Driving wheel diameter* 6 ft. 8 in.; *Boiler pressure* 250 lb.; *Tractive effort at 75% pressure* 31,350 lb.; *Total evap. surface* 2,576 sq. ft.; *Grate area* 41.2 sq. ft.; *Superheating surface* 749 sq. ft.; *Boiler diameter* 6 ft. 5 in./5 ft. 9 in. taper; *Coupled wheelbase* 14 ft. 6 in.; *Engine wheelbase* 35 ft. 9 in.; *Maximum axle load* 22 tons; *Adhesion weight* 66 tons; *Total engine weight* 102.95 tons; *Water capacity* 5,000 gal.; *Coal capacity* 8 tons; *Total wheelbase* 60 ft. $10\frac{5}{8}$ in.; *Total length over buffers* 71 ft. $0\frac{3}{8}$ in.; *Engine and tender weight* 165.35 tons.

L.N.E.R. MIKADOS: These five engines, not all with the same valves and gear, formed an attempt to deal with heavy passenger trains over the steeply-graded and much curved Edinburgh-Aberdeen route. They were cumbrous, awkward, and coal eaters; but the rebuilds into Pacifics were not more successful.

DATA: *Railway* London & North Eastern; *Wheel arrangement* 2–8–2; *Type or class* P2; *Builder* Railway, at Doncaster; *Year built* 1934; *Cyl. (no.) bore and stroke* (3) 21 in. × 26 in.; *Driving wheel diameter* 6 ft. 2 in.; *Boiler pressure* 220 lb.; *Tractive effort at 75% pressure* 38,400 lb.; *Total evap. surface* 2,714 sq. ft.; *Grate area* 50 sq. ft.; *Superheating surface* 635 sq. ft.; *Boiler diameter* 6 ft. 5 in./5 ft. 9 in. taper; *Coupled wheelbase* 19 ft. 6 in.; *Engine wheelbase* 37 ft. 11 in.; *Maximum axle load* 20.5 tons; *Adhesion weight* 80.6 tons; *Total engine weight* 110.2 tons; *Water capacity* 5,000 gal.; *Coal capacity* 8 tons; *Total wheelbase* 64 ft. 0⅞ in.; *Total length over buffers* 73 ft. 8¾ in.; *Engine and tender weight* 165.5 tons.

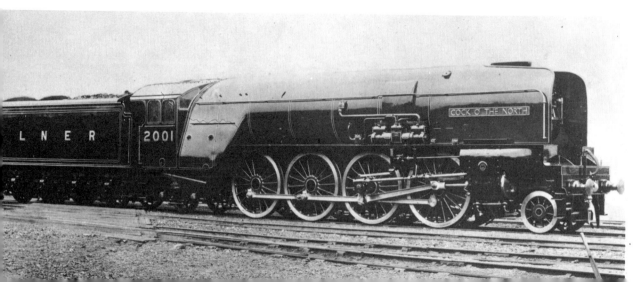

L.N.E.R. GREEN ARROW CLASS: The application of Gresley's big-boiler wide-firebox three-cylinder principles to first-class mixed-traffic needs produced this class of 2–6–2, or Prairie, engine. They were fine traffic shifters on the main lines, and over the 43 per cent of total L.N.E.R. route over which they could run.

DATA: *Railway* London & North Eastern; *Wheel arrangement* 2–6–2; *Type or class* V2; *Builder* Railway, at Doncaster; *Year built* 1936; *Cyl. (no.) bore and stroke* (3) $18\frac{1}{2}$ in. × 26 in.; *Driving wheel diameter* 6 ft. 2 in.; *Boiler pressure* 220 lb.; *Tractive effort at 75% pressure* 29,700 lb.; *Total evap. surface* 2,431 sq. ft.; *Grate area* 41.2 sq. ft.; *Superheating surface* 679 sq. ft.; *Boiler diameter* 6 ft. 5 in./5 ft. 9 in. taper; *Coupled wheelbase* 15 ft. 6 in.; *Engine wheelbase* 33 ft. 8 in.; *Maximum axle load* 22 tons; *Adhesion weight* 65.6 tons; *Total engine weight* 93.1 tons; *Water capacity* 4,200 gal.; *Coal capacity* $7\frac{1}{2}$ tons; *Total wheelbase* 56 ft. $2\frac{1}{8}$ in.; *Total length over buffers* 66 ft. $5\frac{1}{8}$ in.; *Engine and tender weight* 144.1 tons.

L.N.E.R. SPRINGBOKS: This was the war-time and post-war mixed-traffic engine of the L.N.E.R., simple, robust, and with only two cylinders. It could run over 65 per cent of the whole route mileage, and was the L.N.E.R. equivalent of the Black Five on the L.M.S.R.

DATA: *Railway* London & North Eastern; *Wheel arrangement* 4–6–0; *Type or class* B1; *Builder* Railway; NBL; *Years built* 1945–47; *Cyl. (no.) bore and stroke* (2) 20 in. × 26 in.; *Driving wheel diameter* 6 ft. 2 in.; *Boiler pressure* 225 lb.; *Tractive effort at 75% pressure* 23,750 lb.; *Total evap. surface* 1,676 sq. ft.; *Grate area* 27.5 sq. ft.; *Superheating surface* 344 sq. ft.; *Boiler Diameter* 5 ft. 6 in.; *Coupled wheelbase* 16 ft. 3 in.; *Engine wheelbase* 28 ft.; *Maximum axle load* 17.75 tons; *Adhesion weight* 52.5 tons; *Total engine weight* 71.15 tons; *Water capacity* 4,200 gal.; *Coal capacity* 7.5 tons; *Total wheelbase* 51 ft. $2\frac{3}{8}$ in.; *Total length over buffers* 61 ft. $7\frac{3}{8}$ in.; *Engine and tender weight* 123.15 tons.

MIDLAND GOODS: A typical example of the British six-wheel goods locomotive, a type that existed from 1833 to 1968. There were 775 of this Midland/L.M.S.R. class, and at one time they operated numerous excursion and local passenger trains as well as much of the goods traffic.

DATA: *Railway* Midland; and L.M.S.R.; *Wheel arrangement* 0–6–0; *Type or class* 4F; *Builder* Railway; Armstrong Whitworth; *Years built* 1911–22; *Cyl. (no.) bore and stroke* (2) 20 in. × 26 in.; *Driving wheel diameter* 5 ft. 3 in.; *Boiler pressure* 175 lb.; *Tractive effort at 75% pressure* 21,620 lb.; *Total evap. surface* 1,158 sq. ft.; *Grate area* 21 sq. ft.; *Superheating surface* 246 sq. ft.; *Boiler diameter* 4 ft. 8½ in.; *Coupled wheelbase* 16 ft. 6 in.; *Engine wheelbase* 16 ft. 6 in.; *Maximum axle load* 18 tons; *Adhesion weight* 48.75 tons; *Total engine weight* 48.75 tons; *Water capacity* 3,500 gal.; *Coal capacity* 4 tons; *Total wheelbase* 38 ft. 9¼ in.; *Total length over buffers* 52 ft.; *Engine and tender weight* 90 tons.

THE ROYAL SCOTS: The first break-away from the Midland small-engine policy with which the L.M.S.R. was saddled for some years after the Grouping in 1923. The conception was based much on the Southern Railway "Lord Nelson" class, but with three cylinders instead of four.

DATA: *Railway* London, Midland & Scottish; *Wheel arrangement* 4–6–0; *Type or class* Royal Scot; *Builder* North British Loco. Co.; *Year built* 1927; *Cyl. (no.) bore and stroke* (3) 18 in. × 26 in.; *Driving wheel diameter* 6 ft. 9 in.; *Boiler pressure* 250 lb.; *Tractive effort at 75% pressure* 29,400 lb.; *Total evap. surface* 2,081 sq. ft.; *Grate area* 31.2 sq. ft.; *Superheating surface* 399 sq. ft.; *Boiler diameter* 5 ft. 9 in.; *Coupled wheelbase* 15 ft. 4 in.; *Engine wheelbase* 27 ft. 6 in.; *Maximum axle load* 21 tons; *Adhesion weight* 62.5 tons; *Total engine weight* 84.9 tons; *Water capacity* 4,000 gal.; *Coal capacity* 9 tons; *Total wheelbase* 54 ft. 9 in.; *Total length over buffers* 65 ft. 2¾ in.; *Engine and tender weight* 139.65 tons.

STANIER EIGHT-COUPLED ENGINES, L.M.S.R.: Built in hundreds as the standard freight locomotive of the L.M.S.R., this design also formed the basis of the war-time 'Austerity" 2—8—0; and, later still, British Railways made much use of the L.M.S.R.-built engines up to the very end of steam traction.

DATA: *Railway* London, Midland & Scottish; *Wheel arrangement* 2—8—0; *Type or class* 8F; *Builder* Railway, Crewe; *Years built* 1934–48; *Cyl (no.) bore and stroke* (2) 18½ in. × 28 in.; *Driving wheel diameter* 4 ft. 8½ in.; *Boiler pressure* 225 lb.; *Tractive effort at 75% pressure* 28,600 lb.; *Total evap. surface* 1,650 sq. ft.; *Grate area* 28.6 sq. ft.; *Superheating surface* 215 sq. ft.; *Boiler diameter* 5 ft. 8½ in./5 ft. taper; *Coupled wheelbase* 17 ft. 3 in.; *Engine wheelbase* 26 ft.; *Maximum axle load* 16.0 tons; *Adhesion weight* 62 tons; *Total engine weight* 70.5 tons; *Water capacity* 4,000 gal.; *Coal capacity* 9 tons; *Total wheelbase* 52 ft. 7¾ in.; *Total length over buffers* 63 in. 0¾ in.; *Engine and tender weight*; 125.15 tons.

L.M.S. PACIFICS: L.M.S.R. Pacifics began in 1933. The one illustrated was the last of all, and happily named after the man who originated the type 14 years earlier. This last engine had roller bearings and many other detail improvements making for easier maintenance.

DATA: *Railway* London, Midland & Scottish; *Wheel arrangement 4–6–2*; *Type or class* 6256; *Builder* Railway, at Crewe; *Year built* 1947; *Cyl. (no.) bore and stroke* (4) 16.5 in. × 28 in.; *Driving wheel diameter* 6 ft. 9 in.; *Boiler pressure* 250 lb.; *Tractive effort at 75% pressure* 35,300 lb.; *Total evap. surface* 2,807 sq. ft.; *Grate area* 50 sq. ft.; *Superheating surface* 979 sq. ft.; *Boiler diameter* 6 ft. $5\frac{1}{2}$ in./5 ft. $8\frac{1}{2}$ in. taper; *Coupled wheelbase* 14 ft. 6 in.; *Engine wheelbase* 37 ft.; *Maximum axle load* 22.75 tons; *Adhesion weight* 68.1 tons; *Total engine weight* 106.4 tons; *Water capacity* 4,000 gal.; *Coal capacity* 10 tons; *Total wheelbase* 62 ft. 11 in.; *Total length over buffers* 73 ft. $10\frac{1}{4}$ in.; *Engine and tender weight* 163.2 tons.

STANIER BLACK FIVES: This was the celebrated "Black Five", the main-line mixed-traffic engine of the L.M.S.R., built by that company to the end of its existence, and forming the design for the British Railways standard type 5 which perpetuated the colloquial name. The illustration shows one of the last engines built.

DATA: *Railway* London, Midland & Scottish; *Wheel arrangement* 4–6–0; *Type or class* 5P5F; *Builder* Railway, at Crewe; and others; *Years built* 1934–48; *Cyl. (no.) bore and stroke* (2) 18½ in. × 28 in.; *Driving wheel diameter* 6 ft.; *Boiler pressure* 225 lb.; *Tractive effort at 75% pressure* 22,500 lb.; *Total evap. surface* 1,650 sq. ft.; *Grate area* 28.6 sq. ft.; *Superheating surface* 348 sq. ft.; *Boiler diameter* 5 ft. 8½ in./4 ft. 11¾ in. taper; *Coupled wheelbase* 15 ft. 4 in.; *Engine wheelbase* 27 ft. 6 in.; *Maximum axle load* 19.5 tons; *Adhesion weight* 57.3 tons; *Total engine weight* 75.3 tons; *Water capacity* 4,000 gal.; *Coal capacity* 9 tons; *Total wheelbase* 53 ft. 6¾ in.; *Total length over buffers* 63 ft. 11¾ in.; *Engine and tender weight* 129.1 tons.

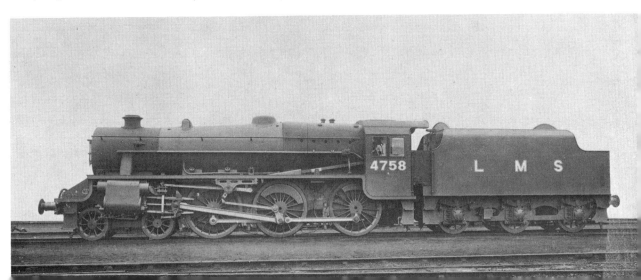

THE LORD NELSONS, S.R.: Haulage of 500 tons along the main lines at an average of 55 m.p.h. was the requirement of this design, which had the four cylinders at a 135-deg. crank arrangement to give eight power impulses per revolution of the wheels. Four sets of valve gear were a feature.

DATA: *Railway* Southern; *Wheel arrangement* 4—6—0; *Type or class* Lord Nelson; *Builder* Railway, at Eastleigh; *Year built* 1925; *Cyl. (no.) bore and stroke* (4) $16\frac{1}{2}$ in. × 26 in.; *Driving wheel diameter* 6 ft. 7 in.; *Boiler pressure* 220 lb.; *Tractive effort at 75% pressure* 29,600 lb.; *Total evap. surface* 1,989 sq. ft.; *Grate area* 33 sq. ft.; *Superheating surface* 376 sq. ft.; *Boiler diameter* 5 ft. 9 in.; *Coupled wheelbase* 15 ft.; *Engine wheelbase* 29 ft. 6 in.; *Maximum axle load* 20.7 tons; *Adhesion weight* 62 tons; *Total engine weight* 83.5 tons; *Water capacity* 5,000 gal.; *Coal capacity* 5 tons; *Total wheelbase* 60 ft. 9 in.; *Total length over buffers* 69 ft. $9\frac{3}{4}$ in.; *Engine and tender weight* 140.2 tons.

THE SOUTHERN SCHOOLS: The most celebrated English 4—4—0 of all—and the heaviest and most powerful—from 1860 to 1960. It was the ''Lord Nelson'' with one pair of coupled wheels and one cylinder subtracted. Astonishing haulage feats were performed on the Bournemouth and Hastings lines.

DATA: *Railway* Southern; *Wheel arrangement* 4—4—0; *Type or class* V; *Builder* Railway, at Eastleigh; *Years built* 1930—31; *Cyl. (no.) bore and stroke* (3) 16½ in. × 26 in.; *Driving wheel diameter* 6 ft. 7 in.; *Boiler pressure* 220 lb.; *Tractive effort at 75% pressure* 22,200 lb.; *Total evap. surface* 1,766 sq. ft.; *Grate area* 28.3 sq. ft.; *Superheating surface* 283 sq. ft.; *Boiler diameter* 5 ft. 5¾ in.; *Coupled wheelbase* 10 ft.; *Engine wheelbase* 25 ft. 6 in.; *Maximum axle load* 21 tons; *Adhesion weight* 42 tons; *Total engine weight* 67.1 tons; *Water capacity* 4,000 gal.; *Coal capacity* 5 tons; *Total wheelbase* 48 ft. 7¼ in.; *Total length over buffers* 58 ft. 9¾ in.; *Engine and tender weight* 109.5 tons.

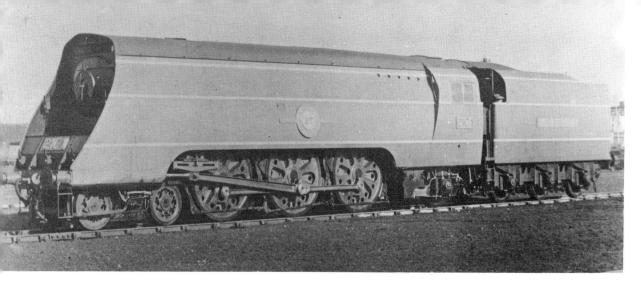

SOUTHERN MERCHANT NAVY CLASS: As "debatable" an engine as the notorious "Ginx's Babies" on the old Stockton & Darlington Railway in 1871–72. They embodied too many new features all at once, and only after rebuilding in British Railways days were the wonderful potentialities produced without daily troubles.

DATA: *Railway* Southern; *Wheel arrangement* 4–6–2; *Type or class* Merchant Navy; *Builder* Railway, at Eastleigh; *Years built* 1941–45; *Cyl. (no.) bore and stroke* (3) 18 in. × 24 in.; *Driving wheel diameter* 6 ft. 2 in.; *Boiler pressure* 280 lb.; *Tractive effort at 75% pressure* 33,000 lb.; *Total evap. surface* 2,451 sq. ft.; *Grate area* 48.5 sq. ft.; *Superheating surface* 822 sq. ft.; *Boiler diameter* 6 ft. 3½ in./5 ft. 8½ in. taper; *Coupled wheelbase* 15 ft.; *Engine wheelbase* 36 ft. 9 in.; *Maximum axle load* 21 tons; *Adhesion weight* 63 tons; *Total engine weight* 94.75 tons; *Water capacity* 5,000 gal.; *Coal capacity* 5 tons; *Total wheelbase* 59 ft. 6 in.; *Total length over buffers* 69 ft. 7¾ in.; *Engine and tender weight* 144.1 tons.

B.R. BRITANNIA PACIFICS: The standard top-class main-line steam passenger power built by British Railways, and the first two-cylinder Pacific in England; all previous 4–6–2 engines had three or four cylinders. They worked on all five Regions. 55 were built, all at Crewe.

DATA: *Railway* British Railways; *Wheel arrangement* 4–6–2; *Type or class* 7P; *Builder* Railway, at Crewe; *Years built* 1951–53; *Cyl. (no.) bore and stroke* (2) 20 in. × 28 in.; *Driving wheel diameter* 6 ft. 2 in.; *Boiler pressure* 250 lb.; *Tractive effort at 75% pressure* 28,400 lb.; *Total evap. surface* 2,474 sq. ft.; *Grate area* 42 sq. ft.; *Superheating surface* 718 sq. ft.; *Boiler diameter* 6 ft. 5½ in./5 ft. 9 in. taper; *Coupled wheelbase* 14 ft.; *Engine wheelbase* 35 ft. 9 in.; *Maximum axle load* 20.3 tons; *Adhesion weight* 60.75 tons; *Total engine weight* 94 tons; *Water capacity* 4,250 gal.; *Coal capacity* 7 tons; *Total wheelbase* 58 ft. 3 in.; *Total length over buffers* 68 ft. 9 in.; *Engine and tender weight* 141.2 tons (with small tender).

B.R. STANDARD LIGHT TANK: This was much the smallest tank engine in the B.R. standard range of engine; it had only limited application, and even this was reduced by the rapid introduction of railcars from 1954. Only 30 were built, and fitted for pull-and-push working.

DATA: *Railway* British Railways; *Wheel arrangement* 2–6–2T; *Type or class* Class 2; *Builder* Railway, at Crewe; *Year built* 1953; *Cyl. (no.) bore and stroke* (2) 16½ in. × 24 in.; *Driving wheel diameter* 5 ft.; *Boiler pressure* 200 lb.; *Tractive effort at 75% pressure* 16,350 lb.; *Total evap. surface* 1,025 sq. ft.; *Grate area* 17.5 sq. ft.; *Superheating surface* 134 sq. ft.; *Boiler diameter* 4 ft. 8 in./4 ft. 3 in. taper; *Coupled wheelbase* 13 ft. 9 in.; *Engine wheelbase* 30 ft. 3 in.; *Maximum axle load* 13 tons; *Adhesion weight* 39 tons; *Total engine weight* 63.25 tons; *Water capacity* 1,350 gal.; *Coal capacity* 3 tons; *Total wheelbase* —; *Total length over buffers* 40 ft.

B.R. STANDARD LIGHT MOGUL: The second smallest tender engine among the 12 tender and tank types projected by British Railways, and designed as a substitute for old 0–6–0s of light axle load which were worn out; but only 20 were built.

DATA: *Railway* British Railways; *Wheel arrangement* 2–6–0; *Type or class* Class 3; *Builder* Railway, at Swindon; *Year built* 1954; *Cyl. (no.) bore and stroke* (2) 17½ in. × 26 in.; *Driving wheel diameter* 5 ft. 3 in.; *Boiler pressure* 200 lb.; *Tractive effort at 75% pressure* 19,100 lb.; *Total evap. surface* 1,051 sq. ft.; *Grate area* 20.3 sq. ft.; *Superheating surface* 190 sq. ft.; *Boiler diameter* 5 ft. 0½ in./4 ft. 5 in. taper; *Coupled wheelbase* 15 ft. 4 in.; *Engine wheelbase* 24 ft. 1 in.; *Maximum axle load* 16.6 tons; *Adhesion weight* 48.5 tons; *Total engine weight* 57.5 tons; *Water capacity* 3,500 gal.; *Coal capacity* 6 tons; *Total wheelbase* 46 ft. 11¾ in.; *Total length over buffers* 55 ft. 11¼ in.; *Engine and tender weight* 99.65 tons.

B.R. TYPE 9 FREIGHT ENGINES: These 251 engines formed the last class of steam locomotive produced by British Railways. Last of all was No. 92220, named *Evening Star*. Ten engines had the curious Franco-Crosti boiler with inbuilt feed water heater; a few others had mechanical stokers.

DATA: *Railway* British Railways; *Wheel arrangement* 2–10–0; *Type or class* 9F; *Builder* Railway; *Years built* 1954–59; *Cyl. (no.) bore and stroke* (2) 20 in. × 28 in.; *Driving wheel diameter* 5 ft; *Boiler pressure* 250 lb.; *Tractive effort at 75% pressure* 35,000 lb.; *Total evap. surface* 2,015 sq. ft.; *Grate area* 40.2 sq. ft.; *Superheating surface* 535 sq. ft.; *Boiler diameter* 6 ft. 1 in./5 ft. 9 in. taper; *Coupled wheelbase* 21 ft. 8 in.; *Engine wheelbase* 30 ft. 2 in.; *Maximum axle load* 15.5 tons; *Adhesion weight* 77.5 tons; *Total engine weight* 86.7 tons; *Water capacity* 5,625 gal.; *Coal capacity* 7 tons; *Total wheelbase* 55 ft. 11 in.; *Total length over buffers* 66 ft. 2 in.; *Engine and tender weight* 142 tons.

IRISH COMPOUNDS: These were the last three-cylinder compounds built for service in the British Isles. After World War II they were supplemented by five similar engines but with three high-pressure cylinders. There was little to choose between the two, and both classes did fine work on the 5 ft. 3 in. gauge Dublin-Belfast line.

DATA: *Railway* G.N.R. (Ireland); *Wheel arrangement* 4–4–0; *Type or class* 3 c.c.; *Builder* Beyer Peacock; *Year built* 1932; *Cyl. (no.) bore and stroke* (1) 17.25 in. × 26 in. h.p.; (2) 19 in. × 26 in. l.p.; *Driving wheel diameter* 6 ft. 7 in.; *Boiler pressure* 250 lb.; *Tractive effort at 75% pressure* 22,000 lb.; *Total evap. surface* 1,251 sq. ft.; *Grate area* 25.2 sq. ft.; *Superheating surface* 276 sq. ft.; *Boiler diameter* 5 ft. 1½ in.; *Coupled wheelbase* 10 ft. 8 in.; *Engine wheelbase* 24 ft. 9 in.; *Maximum axle load* 21 tons; *Adhesion weight* 41 tons; *Total engine weight* 65.1 tons; *Water capacity* 3,500 gal.; *Coal capacity* 6 tons; *Total wheelbase* 45 ft. 8 in.; *Total length over buffers* 55 ft. 3½ in.; *Engine and tender weight* 103.55 tons.

ENGERTH SEMI-ARTICULATED TYPE: The Engerth was a curious design popular last century in Austria, France and Belgium. Originally the axles of the trailing bogie were driven by gears from the hind driving axle, so that the full locomotive weight was adhesive, but the gears were soon taken out, and the engine became just a cumbersome tank engine.

DATA: *Railway* Austrian Karst; *Wheel arrangement* 0–4–6T; *Type or class* Engerth; *Builder* MF Esslingen; *Years built* 1856–57; *Cyl. (no.) bore and stroke* (2) 16.55 in. × 22.8 in.; *Driving wheel diameter* 5 ft. 3 in.; *Boiler pressure* 100 lb.; *Tractive effort at 75% pressure* 7,460 lb.; *Total evap. surface* 1,175 sq. ft.; *Grate area* 12.75 sq. ft.; *Superheating surface* Nil; *Boiler diameter* 3 ft. 2 in.; *Coupled wheelbase* 8 ft. 10½ in.; *Engine wheelbase* 23 ft. 8 in.; *Maximum axle load* 10.5 tons; *Adhesion weight* 21 tons; *Total engine weight* 45 tons; *Water capacity* 1,320 gal.; *Coal capacity* 1.2 tons; *Total wheelbase* —; *Total length over buffers* 34 ft. 11 in.

AUSTRIAN 12-COUPLED COMPOUND: The first 12-coupled tender engine to run in Europe, but it was not repeated on the Austrian State Railways. Built for the Arlberg line and its long 1 in 40 gradients, No. 100.01 was the largest of the many Gölsdorf four-cylinder compounds of numerous wheel arrangements.

DATA: *Railway* Austrian State; *Wheel arrangement* 2–12–0; *Type or class* 100; *Builder* Floridsdorf; *Year built* 1911; *Cyl. (no.) bore and stroke* (2) 17.75 in. × 26.75 in. h.p.; (2) 29.87 in. × 26.75 in. l.p.; *Driving wheel diameter* 4 ft. 9 in.; *Boiler pressure* 235 lb.; *Tractive effort at 75% pressure* 56,000 lb.; *Total evap. surface* 2.573 sq. ft.; *Grate area* 53.8 sq. ft.; *Superheating surface* 613 sq. ft.; *Boiler diameter* 6 ft./5 ft. 7 in. taper; *Coupled wheelbase* 26 ft. 3 in.; *Engine wheelbase* 34 ft. 5 in.; *Maximum axle load* 13.7 tons; *Adhesion weight* 82 tons; *Total engine weight* 94.25 tons; *Water capacity* 3,500 gal.; *Coal capacity* 5 tons; *Total wheelbase* 55 ft.; *Total length over buffers* 66 ft. 6 in.; *Engine and tender weight* 133 tons.

NORWEGIAN PASSENGER ENGINES: Very light permissible axle load was a feature of Norwegian main lines in steam traction days. These 30a-class engines had only 13¾ tons, but they had four cylinders; later 4-cylinder compound 4—6—0s were built, and then 4—8—0 engines, which were allowed 14.3 tons per axle.

DATA: *Railway* Norwegian State; *Wheel arrangement* 4—6—0; *Type or class* 30a; *Builder* Thunes Mekaniska; *Years built* 1914—19; *Cyl. (no.) bore and stroke* (4) 15.35 in. × 23.6 in.; *Driving wheel diameter* 5 ft. 3 in.; *Boiler pressure* 185 lb.; *Tractive effort at 75% pressure* 24,400 lb.; *Total evap. surface* 1,475 sq. ft.; *Grate area* 25.9 sq. ft.; *Superheating surface* 355 sq. ft.; *Boiler diameter* 5 ft. 3 in.; *Coupled wheelbase* 11 ft. 10 in.; *Engine wheelbase* 25 ft. 5 in.; *Maximum axle load* 13.7 tons; *Adhesion weight* 41.1 tons; *Total engine weight* 60.2 tons; *Water capacity* 3,300 gal.; *Coal capacity* 4 tons; *Total wheelbase* 48 ft. 7 in.; *Total length over buffers* 58 ft.; *Engine and tender weight* 95.8 tons.

SPANISH BROAD-GAUGE MOUNTAIN ENGINES: Bridges set a strict limit to the weight per unit of length, and so, despite the low axle load of 16 tons, the length had to be spread out far beyond the leading bogie. Compound propulsion was quite common in Spain at the time these engines were built. Rail gauge 5 ft. 6 in.

DATA: *Railway* Northern of Spain; *Wheel arrangement* 4–8–2; *Type or class* 4600; *Builder* Hanomag, etc.; *Years built* 1925–30; *Cyl. (no.) bore and stroke* (2) 18.1 in. × 26.8 in. h.p.; (2) 27.6 in. × 26.8 in. l.p.; *Driving wheel diameter* 5 ft. 9 in.; *Boiler pressure* 235 lb.; *Tractive effort at 75% pressure* 32,000 lb.; *Total evap. surface* 2,609 sq. ft.; *Grate area* 53.8 sq. ft.; *Superheating surface* 827 sq. ft.; *Boiler diameter* 6 ft. 5 in./5 ft. 9 in. taper; *Coupled wheelbase* 18 ft. 3 in.; Engine wheelbase 41 ft. 7 in.; *Maximum axle load* 16 tons; *Adhesion weight* 64 tons; *Total engine weight* 103 tons; *Water capacity* 5,500 gal.; *Coal capacity* 6 tons; *Total wheelbase* 69 ft. 9 in.; *Total length over buffers* 83 ft. 9 in.; *Engine and tender weight* 163 tons.

GERMAN HEAVY DECAPODS: More than 1,000 of these powerful three-cylinder engines were built for the Reichsbahn after a year or two of tests had shown it was better than the corresponding two-cylinder version. Quite a number were still at work in 1969, taking 1,500-ton goods trains with ease.

DATA: *Railway* German State; *Wheel arrangement* 2–10–0; *Type or class* 44; *Builder* Henschel and others; *Years built* 1926–43; *Cyl. (no.) bore and stroke* (3) 21.6 in. × 26 in.; *Driving wheel diameter* 4 ft. 7 in.; *Boiler pressure* 227 lb.; *Tractive effort at 75% pressure* 56,000 lb.; *Total evap. surface* 2,741 sq. ft.; *Grate area* 50.6 sq. ft.; *Superheating surface* 965 sq. ft.; *Boiler diameter* 6 ft. 3 in.; *Coupled wheelbase* 22 ft. 4 in.; *Engine wheelbase* 31 ft. 8 in.; *Maximum axle load* 19.7 tons; *Adhesion weight* 94 tons; *Total engine weight* 109 tons; *Water capacity* 7,050 gal.; *Coal capacity* 10 tons; *Total wheelbase* 63 ft.; *Total length over buffers* 74 ft. 2½ in.; *Engine and tender weight* 183 tons.

FIRST P.L.M. 4–8–2 ENGINES: The first batches of these lengthy engines had the drive from the outside cylinders on to the leading coupled axle; in later engines the drive was on to the second axle by longer connecting rods. All were four-cylinder compounds, but with only one set of reversing gear.

DATA: *Railway* Paris, Lyons & Mediterranean; *Wheel arrangement* 4–8–2; *Type or class* 241.A; *Builder* Schneider; AFL; *Years built* 1925–31; *Cyl. (no.) bore and stroke* (2) 20 in. × 25.6 in. h.p.; (2) 28.3 in. × 27.5 in. l.p.; *Driving wheel diameter* 5 ft. 11 in.; *Boiler pressure* 227 lb.; *Tractive effort at 75% pressure* 24,500 lb.; *Total evap. surface* 2,645 sq. ft.; *Grate area* 53.8 sq. ft.; *Superheating surface* 932 sq. ft.; *Boiler diameter* 6 ft.; *Coupled wheelbase* 19 ft. 2½ in.; *Engine wheelbase* 43 ft.; *Maximum axle load* 18.5 tons; *Adhesion weight* 73 tons; *Total engine weight* 112.5 tons; *Water capacity* 6,160 gal.; *Coal capacity* 7 tons; *Total wheelbase* 70 ft. 6 in.; *Total length over buffers* 82 ft.; *Engine and tender weight* 173.5 tons.

ITALIAN EXPRESS PACIFICS: Few Pacific engines were used in Italy, as 2–6–2 engines could handle most of the passenger trains. But on the level Turin-Milan-Venice line higher speeds were permitted, and two classes of Pacific in all were utilised, of which Group 691 was the most successful.

DATA: *Railway* Italian State; *Wheel arrangement* 4–6–2; *Type or class* 691; *Builder* Railway, at Florence; *Year built* 1928; *Cyl. (no.) bore and stroke* (4) 17.7 in. × 26.75 in.; *Driving wheel diameter* 6 ft. 8 in.; *Boiler pressure* 200 lb.; *Tractive effort at 75% pressure* 32,550 lb.; *Total evap. surface* 2,632 sq. ft.; *Grate area* 46.2 sq. ft.; *Superheating surface* 1,030 sq. ft.; *Boiler diameter* 6 ft./5 ft. 6 in. taper; *Coupled wheelbase* 14 ft. 1¼ in.; *Engine wheelbase* 35 ft. 11 in.; *Maximum axle load* 19.7 tons; *Adhesion weight* 59 tons; *Total engine weight* 93 tons; *Water capacity* 7,050 gal.; *Coal capacity* 7 tons; *Total wheelbase* 64 ft. 9 in.; *Total length over buffers* 74 ft. 5¾ in.; *Engine and tender weight* 159 tons.

M.Z.A. EIGHT-COUPLED PASSENGER ENGINES: Until well after World War II no railway in Spain could take anything like a 20-ton axle load, and so eight-coupled engines were quite common for passenger trains. The 4–8–0 was a favourite, and the later models were all simple-expansion like this two-cylinder M.Z.A. engine. Rail gauge 5 ft. 6 in.

DATA: *Railway* Madrid, Zaragossa & Alicante; *Wheel arrangement* 4–8–0; *Type or class* 1536; *Builder* Maquinista; *Years built* 1929–30; *Cyl. (no.) bore and stroke* (2) 24.4 in. × 26 in.; *Driving wheel diameter* 5 ft. 3 in.; *Boiler pressure* 200 lb.; *Tractive effort at 75% pressure* 36,800 lb.; *Total evap. surface* 2,350 sq. ft.; *Grate area* 49 sq. ft.; *Superheating surface* 436 sq. ft.; *Boiler diameter* 5 ft. 9 in.; *Coupled wheelbase* 18 ft. 8 in.; *Engine wheelbase* 31 ft. 3½ in.; *Maximum axle load* 17 tons; *Adhesion weight* 66.5 tons; *Total engine weight* 89.5 tons; *Water capacity* 5,500 gal.; *Coal capacity* 6 tons; *Total wheelbase* 58 ft. 5 in.; *Total length over buffers* 68 ft. 2½ in.; *Engine and tender weight* 145 tons.

CZECHOSLOVAK PACIFICS: One of the most elegant Pacifics built in Europe, this class was built to very moderate axle load; and with bar frames and certain other American practices they began a new line in Czechoslovak engines which remained until the end of steam traction, and included fine 4-8-2 and 4-8-4T types.

DATA: *Railway* Czechoslovak State; *Wheel arrangement* 4-6-2; *Type or class* 387; *Builder* Skoda; *Years built* 1928-32; *Cyl. (no.) bore and stroke* (3) 20.6 in. × 26.75 in.; *Driving wheel diameter* 6 ft. 1 in.; *Boiler pressure* 185 lb.; *Tractive effort at 75% pressure* 32,500 lb.; *Total evap. surface* 2,412 sq. ft.; *Grate area* 51.6 sq. ft.; *Superheating surface* 693 sq. ft.; *Boiler diameter* 6 ft. 1 in.; *Coupled wheelbase* 13 ft. 5½ in.; *Engine wheelbase* 36 ft. 1 in.; *Maximum axle load* 17 tons; *Adhesion weight* 51 tons; *Total engine weight* 90.5 tons; *Water capacity* 5,000 gal.; *Coal capacity* 8 tons; *Total wheelbase* 64 ft. 5¾ in.; *Total length over buffers* 76 ft. 1¼ in.; *Engine and tender weight* 146 tons.

BELGIAN CONSOLIDATIONS: These engines began the heavy axle-load era in Belgium—with an increase of 15 per cent. Thereafter 23-ton loads were common for new main-line engines, mainly 2–8–2, 4–6–2 and streamlined 4–4–2 classes, most with high piston loads like the 45 tons of this Consolidation.

DATA: *Railway* Belgian National; *Wheel arrangement* 2–8–0; *Type or class* 35; *Builder* Cockerill; *Years built* 1929–30; *Cyl. (no.) bore and stroke* (2) 25.6 in. × 28.35 in.; *Driving wheel diameter* 4 ft. 9 in.; *Boiler pressure* 200 lb.; *Tractive effort at 75% pressure* 48,560 lb.; *Total evap. surface* 2,502 sq. ft.; *Grate area* 54.6 sq. ft.; *Superheating surface* 730 sq. ft.; *Boiler diameter* 6 ft. 5 in.; *Coupled wheelbase* 19 ft. 2$\frac{1}{4}$ in.; *Engine wheelbase* 27 ft. 10$\frac{1}{2}$ in.; *Maximum axle load* 23 tons; *Adhesion weight* 90.2 tons; *Total engine weight* 105 tons; *Water capacity* 5,280 gal.; *Coal capacity* 7 tons; *Total wheelbase* 52 ft. 9$\frac{3}{4}$ in.; *Total length over buffers* 64 ft. 5$\frac{1}{4}$ in.; *Engine and tender weight* 157.75 tons.

EXPRESS ENGINES IN HOLLAND: The most powerful passenger engines ever to run in Holland. Boilers, cylinders and other details were the same as in some enormous 4–8–4T engines for coal trains, and both classes were built up on bar frames. There are very few steep gradients in Holland.

DATA: *Railway* Netherlands; *Wheel arrangement* 4–6–0; *Type or class* PO 4 (3900); *Builder* Henschel; *Years built* 1929–30; *Cyl. (no.) bore and stroke* (4) $16\frac{1}{2}$ in. × 26 in.; *Driving wheel diameter* 6 ft. $1\frac{3}{4}$ in.; *Boiler pressure* 206 lb.; *Tractive effort at 75% pressure* 29,550 lb.; *Total evap. surface* 1,949 sq. ft.; *Grate area* 34 sq. ft.; *Superheating surface* 485 sq. ft.; *Boiler diameter* 5 ft. $6\frac{1}{2}$ in.; *Coupled wheelbase* 14 ft. $9\frac{1}{4}$ in.; *Engine wheelbase* 30 ft. 8 in.; *Maximum axle load* 18.2 tons; *Adhesion weight* 54.1 tons; *Total engine weight* 82.7 tons; *Water capacity* 6,160 gal.; *Coal capacity* 6 tons; *Total wheelbase* 55 ft. 10 in.; *Total length over buffers* 66 ft. $11\frac{1}{2}$ in.; *Engine and tender weight* 144.7 tons.

AUSTRIAN 2–8–4 PASSENGER ENGINES: No more than 14 of these magnificent smooth-riding engines were built in Austria because of approaching electrification of the main lines that could take them; but the design was used in Bucharest for more than 70 engines built for the Roumanian State Railways.

DATA: *Railway* Austrian Federal; *Wheel arrangement* 2–8–4; *Type or class* 214; *Builder* Floridsdorf; *Years built* 1929–34; *Cyl. (no.) bore and stroke* (2) 25.6 in. × 28.4 in.; *Driving wheel diameter* 6 ft. 4½ in.; *Boiler pressure* 214 lb.; *Tractive effort at 75% pressure* 40,000 lb.; *Total evap. surface* 3,057 sq. ft.; *Grate area* 50.8 sq. ft.; *Superheating surface* 880 sq. ft.; *Boiler diameter* 6 ft. 3½ in.; *Coupled wheelbase* 20 ft. 4½ in.; *Engine wheelbase* 41 ft. 5½ in.; *Maximum axle load* 17.75 tons; *Adhesion weight* 70.5 tons; *Total engine weight* 116.1 tons; *Water capacity* 5,940 gal.; *Coal capacity* 8 tons; *Total wheelbase* 64 ft. 4 in.; *Total length over buffers* 75 ft. 8 in.; *Engine and tender weight* 171.3 tons.

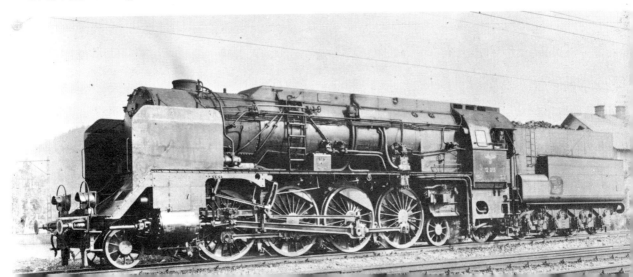

FRENCH DECAPODS FOR COAL TRAINS: This design for mineral-train haulage in the Lorraine area was drawn up after experience with both French and German 10-coupled engines; its three big cylinders and high adhesion weight gave great hauling power at low speeds.

DATA: *Railway* Eastern of France; *Wheel arrangement* 2–10–0; *Type or class* XIII; *Builder* Fives-Lille, etc.; *Years built* 1926–32; *Cyl. (no.) bore and stroke* (3) 22 in. × 26 in.; *Driving wheel diameter* 4 ft. 7 in.; *Boiler pressure* 200 lb.; *Tractive effort at 75% pressure* 51,500 lb.; *Total evap. surface* 2,339 sq. ft.; *Grate area* 35 sq. ft.; *Superheating surface* 730 sq. ft.; *Boiler diameter* 6 ft. 1 in.; *Coupled wheelbase* 20 ft. 4¼ in.; *Engine wheelbase* 30 ft. 4¾ in.; *Maximum axle load* 16.5 tons; *Adhesion weight* 70.5 tons; *Total engine weight* 116.1 tons; *Weight capacity* 5,940 gal.; *Coal capacity* 8 tons; *Total wheelbase* 63 ft.; *Total length over buffers* 74 ft. 9 in.; *Engine and tender weight* 166 tons.

AUSTRIAN SINGLE-DRIVER TANK: This unusual little tank engine was a rebuild of a still earlier machine, to check whether a small "single driver" could work economically light local and branch-line trains. After World War II it was converted into a special bridge-testing locomotive, and no more used in regular traffic.

DATA: *Railway* Austrian Federal; *Wheel arrangement* 2—2—2T; *Type or class* 12; *Builder* Floridsdorf; *Year built* 1934; *Cyl. (no.) bore and stroke* (2) 13.6 in. × 18.9 in.; *Driving wheel diameter* 4 ft. 7½ in.; *Boiler pressure* 156 lb.; *Tractive effort at 75% pressure* 7,400 lb.; *Total evap. surface* 635 sq. ft.; *Grate area* 11 sq. ft.; *Superheating surface* Nil; *Boiler diameter* 3 ft. 4½ in.; *Coupled wheelbase* Nil; *Engine wheelbase* 10 ft. 10½ in.: *Maximum axle load* 13 tons; *Adhesion weight* 13 tons; *Total engine weight* 32 tons; *Water capacity* 880 gal.; *Coal capacity* 1 ton; *Total wheelbase* —; *Total length over buffers* 26 ft.

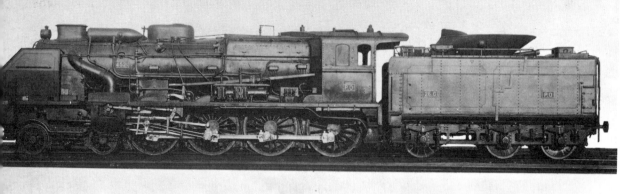

EUROPE'S MOST POWERFUL STEAM LOCOMOTIVE: Of all steam locomotives built over 150 years, these eight-coupled Chapelon rebuilds showed the highest output per unit of weight—39 indicated h.p. per ton, or 4,170 i.h.p. from 107 tons of locomotive weight. They handled express passenger trains up to 900–1,000 tons.

DATA: *Railway* Paris-Orleans; *Wheel arrangement* 4–8–0; *Type or class* 4701; *Builder* Railway, at Tours; *Years built* 1932–34; *Cyl. (no.) bore and stroke* (2) 17.4 in. × 25.6 in. h.p.; (2) 25.2 in. × 25.6 in. l.p.; *Driving wheel diameter* 6 ft. 1 in.; *Boiler pressure* 290 lb.; *Tractive effort at 75% pressure* 33,500 lb.; *Total evap. surface* 2,300 sq. ft.; *Grate area* 40.5 sq. ft.; *Superheating surface* 720 sq. ft.; *Boiler diameter* 6 ft. 1 in./5 ft. 8 in. taper; *Coupled wheelbase* 19 ft. 8¾ in.; *Engine wheelbase* 32 ft. 10 in.; *Maximum axle load* 19 tons; *Adhesion weight* 75.2 tons; *Total engine weight* 107 tons; *Water capacity* 5,700 gal.; *Coal capacity* 8.8 tons; *Total wheelbase* 57 ft. 2 in.; *Total length over buffers* 66 ft. 10½ in.; *Engine and tender weight* 163.8 tons.

BELGIAN FOUR-CYLINDER PACIFICS: Though not the first Pacifics in Belgium, these were the most successful, and also the most powerful passenger locomotives to run in the country, and operated the three principal main lines until superseded by electric and diesel units.

DATA: *Railway* Belgian National; *Wheel arrangement* 4–6–2; *Type or class* Type 1; *Builder* Tubize; Cockerill; *Year built* 1936; *Cyl. (no.) bore and stroke* (4) 16.5 in. × 28.4 in.; *Driving wheel diameter* 6 ft. 6 in.; *Boiler pressure* 256 lb.; *Tractive effort at 75% pressure* 38,000 lb.; *Total evap. surface* 2,527 sq. ft.; *Grate area* 54 sq. ft.; *Superheating surface* 1,202 sq. ft.; *Boiler diameter* 6 ft. 2 in./5 ft. 10 in. taper; *Coupled wheelbase* 13 ft. 5 in.; *Engine wheelbase* 37 ft. 6 in.; *Maximum axle load* 24 tons; *Adhesion weight* 71 tons; *Total engine weight* 124 tons; *Water capacity* 8,360 gal.; *Coal capacity* 8.25 tons; *Total wheelbase* 68 ft. 10 in.; *Total length over buffers* 79 ft. 10 in.; *Engine and tender weight* 204 tons.

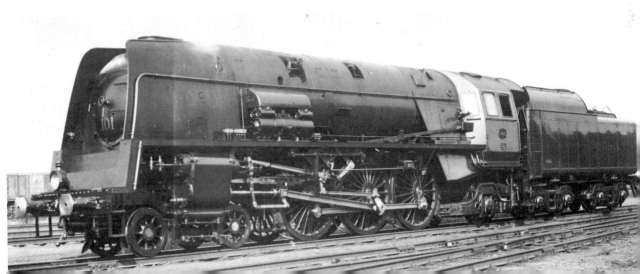

GERMAN STANDARD THREE-CYLINDER PACIFIC: Within the completely new range of standard locomotives introduced in Germany in 1925–27 were Pacifics (type 01) with 20-ton axle load. Later these were supplemented by type 03 with 18½-ton axle load and three cylinders, and some of these are still (1969) at work.

DATA: *Railway* German State; *Wheel arrangement* 4–6–2; *Type or class* 03[10]; *Builder* Various; *Years built* 1937–40; *Cyl. (no.) bore and stroke* (3) 18.5 in. × 26 in.; *Driving wheel diameter* 6 ft. 6¾ in.; *Boiler pressure* 227 lb.; *Tractive effort at 75% pressure* 28,900 lb.; *Total evap. surface* 2,185 sq. ft.; *Grate area* 42 sq. ft.; *Superheating surface* 775 sq. ft.; *Boiler diameter* 5 ft. 7 in.; *Coupled wheelbase* 14 ft. 9 in.; *Engine wheelbase* 39 ft. 4½ in.; *Maximum axle load* 18.5 tons; *Adhesion weight* 55 tons; *Total engine weight* 103 tons; *Water capacity* 7,500 gal.; *Coal capacity* 10 tons; *Total wheelbase* 66 ft. 6 in.; *Total length over buffers* 78 ft. 5 in.; *Engine and tender weight* 177.5 tons.

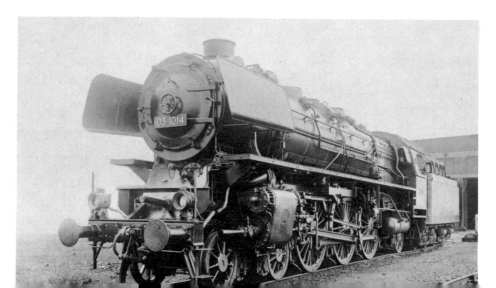

TWELVE-COUPLED RACK-AND-ADHESION TANK: Culmination of the rack-and-adhesion locomotives on the well-known Eisenerz mineral rack railway in Austria was two of these "ironclads". Previous designs had been 0—6—2T and 0—12—OT, and they are still in existence, whereas the newer 2—12—Ts have been withdrawn as too cumbrous.

DATA: *Railway* Austrian Federal; *Wheel arrangement* 2—12—2T; *Type or class* 97[4]; *Builder* Floridsdorf; *Year built* 1941; *Cyl. (no.) bore and stroke* (2) 24 in. × 20.5 in. (adhesion); (2) 15.75 in. × 19.7 in. (rack); *Driving wheel diameter* 3 ft. 5½ in.; *Boiler pressure* 227 lb.; *Tractive effort at 75% pressure* 48,400 lb. (adhesion); *Total evap. surface* 2,264 sq. ft.; *Grate area* 42 sq. ft.; *Superheating surface* 780 sq. ft.; *Boiler diameter* 5 ft. 6 in.; *Coupled wheelbase* 22 ft. 10 in.; *Engine wheelbase* 37 ft. 7 in.; *Maximum axle load* 16.5 tons; *Adhesion weight* 96.4 tons; *Total engine weight* 123.6 tons; *Water capacity* 2,100 gal.; *Coal capacity* 3.5 tons; *Total wheelbase* —; *Total length over buffers* 48 ft. 2 in.

GERMAN "AUSTERITY" LOCOMOTIVE: More than 8,000 of these engines were built within 5 years of their introduction in 1941. They were the German war-time "Austerity" locomotives, using almost no materials then in short supply, and economising in production man-hours. Some had large condensing tenders, and a smokebox draught by fan.

DATA: *Railway* German Federal; *Wheel arrangement* 2–10–0; *Type or class* 52 (or "Austerity"); *Builder* Numerous; *Years built* 1941–47; *Cyl. (no.) bore and stroke* (2) 23.6 in. × 26 in.; *Driving wheel diameter* 4 ft. 7 in.; *Boiler pressure* 227 lb.; *Tractive effort at 75% pressure* 45,000 lb.; *Total evap. surface* 1,919 sq. ft.; *Grate area* 42 sq. ft.; *Superheating surface* 682 sq. ft.; *Boiler diameter* 5 ft. 7 in.; *Coupled wheelbase* 21 ft. 8 in.; *Engine wheelbase* 30 ft. 3 in.; *Maximum axle load* 15 tons; *Adhesion weight* 73.5 tons; *Total engine weight* 83.25 tons; *Water capacity* 6,600 gal.; *Coal capacity* 10 tons; *Total wheelbase* 62 ft.; *Total length over buffers* 75 ft. 5 in.; *Engine and tender weight* 140.85 tons.

FRENCH SIX-CYLINDER 12-COUPLED COMPOUND: This one remarkable six-cylinder machine, with two high-pressure and four low-pressure cylinders, was built to show how high a thermal efficiency might be given by a steam locomotive. It had a superheater, re-superheater and feed water heater, but came too late to give steam traction a further chance against electrics and diesels.

DATA: *Railway* French National; *Wheel arrangement* 2–12–0; *Type or class* 160.A1; *Builder* Railway; *Year built* 1948; *Cyl. (no.) bore and stroke* (2) 20.5 in. × 21.2 in. h.p.; (2) 25.2 in. × 25.6 in. l.p.; (2) 20.5 in. × 21.2 in. l.p.; *Driving wheel diameter* 4 ft. 7 in.; *Boiler pressure* 260 lb.; *Tractive effort at 75% pressure* 80,000 lb.; *Total evap. surface* 2,346 sq. ft.; *Grate area* 47.4 sq. ft.; *Superheating surface* 775 sq. ft. + 1,098 sq. ft. resuperheater; *Boiler diameter* 6 ft.; *Coupled wheelbase* 27 ft. 4 in.; *Engine wheelbase* 35 ft. 4½ in.; *Maximum axle load* 19.8 tons; *Adhesion weight* 118.1 tons; *Total engine weight* 135.35 tons; *Water capacity* 7,700 gal.; *Coal capacity* 9 tons; *Total wheelbase* 70 ft. 4 in.; *Total length over buffers* 82 ft. 6 in.; *Engine and tender weight* 212 tons.

GERMAN POST-WAR PASSENGER STANDARD: After World War II the German Federal Railway, though largely committed to electric and diesel traction, built three new standard steam locomotive types, 2–6–2, 2–8–4T and 0–10–0T. All had the outstanding feature of a fully-welded boiler, without rivets or screwed stays.

DATA: *Railway* German Federal; *Wheel arrangement* 2–6–2; *Type or class* 23; *Builder* Various; *Years built* 1951–55; *Cyl. (no.) bore and stroke* (2) 20.5 in. × 26 in.; *Driving wheel diameter* 5 ft. 9 in.; *Boiler pressure* 200 lb.; *Tractive effort at 75% pressure* 23,800 lb.; *Total evap. surface* 1,681 sq. ft.; *Grate area* 33.5 sq. ft.; *Superheating surface* 794 sq. ft.; *Boiler diameter* 6 ft.; *Coupled wheelbase* 13 ft. 2 in.; *Engine wheelbase* 32 ft. 6 in.; *Maximum axle load* 17 tons; *Adhesion weight* 51 tons; *Total engine weight* 80 tons; *Water capacity* 6,800 gal.; *Coal capacity* 7.75 tons; *Total wheelbase* 55 ft. 6 in.; *Total length over buffers* 70 ft.; *Engine and tender weight* 145 tons.

GREEK MAIN-LINE 2–10–2: Built as part of Italian war reparations to Greece, these 20 engines were the last large steam locomotives built for service in Europe. Despite the long 1 in 40–50 gradients between Athens and Salonika, they were really too large and complicated, and have now been replaced by diesels.

DATA: *Railway* Greek State; *Wheel arrangement* 2–10–2; *Type or class* 1011; *Builder* Breda and Ansaldo; *Year built* 1954; *Cyl. (no.) bore and stroke* (2) 26 in. × 27.5 in.; *Driving wheel diameter* 5 ft. 3 in.; *Boiler pressure* 256 lb.; *Tractive effort at 75% pressure* 56,400 lb.; *Total evap. surface* 3,359 sq. ft.; *Grate area* 60.3 sq. ft.; *Superheating surface* 1,346 sq. ft.; *Boiler diameter* 6 ft. 10½ in.; *Coupled wheelbase* 23 ft.; *Engine wheelbase* 42 ft.; *Maximum axle load* 20 tons; *Adhesion weight* 100 tons; *Total engine weight* 132 tons; *Water capacity* 5,500 gal.; *Coal capacity* 12 tons; *Total wheelbase* 71 ft. 6 in.; *Total length over buffers* 81 ft. 1 in.; *Engine and tender weight* 195 tons.

SOVIET STANDARD FREIGHT ENGINE: The most numerous class of steam locomotive ever; something like 13,000 were built in six or seven sub-types over 40 years by nearly 30 builders in five countries for the Russian and Soviet railway system. Certain main dimensions such as cylinder size, wheel diameter, and wheelbase remained unchanged throughout.
DATA: *Railway* U.S.S.R.; *Wheel arrangement* 0–10–0; *Type or class* E; *Builder* Various Russian, German, Swedish; *Years built* 1912–52; *Cyl. (no.) bore and stroke* (2) 25.6 in. × 27.6 in.; *Driving wheel diameter* 4 ft. 4 in.; *Boiler pressure* 170/200 lb.; *Tractive effort at 75% pressure* 44,400 lb. (at 170 lb.); *Total evap. surface* 2,231 sq. ft.; *Grate area* 48 sq. ft.; *Superheating surface* 547 sq. ft.; *Boiler diameter* 5 ft. 8 in.; *Coupled wheelbase* 18 ft. 11½ in.; *Engine wheelbase* 18 ft. 11½ in.; *Maximum axle load* 17 tons; *Adhesion weight* 84 tons; *Total engine weight* 84 tons; *Water capacity* 5,050 gal.; *Coal capacity* 5.7 tons; *Total wheelbase* 52 ft.; *Total length over buffers* 67 ft.; *Engine and tender weight* 136 tons.

NORTH AFRICAN EXPRESS BEYER-GARRATT: Complete rejuvenation of the Algerian main-line system in the 1930s included these express articulated locomotives for the main Algiers-Constantine and Algiers-Oran services. They ran regularly up to 70 m.p.h. They had special Cossart valve gear, and enclosed circular coal bunkers.

DATA: *Railway* Algerian; *Wheel arrangement* 4-6-2 + 2-6-4; *Type or class* 231-132 BT; *Builder* Soc. Franco-Belge; *Years built* 1938-39; *Cyl. (no.) bore and stroke* (4) 19.3 in. × 26 in.; *Driving wheel diameter* 6 ft. 2 in.; *Boiler pressure* 285 lb.; *Tractive effort at 75% pressure* 56,000 lb.; *Total evap. surface* 2,800 sq. ft.; *Grate area* 59.6 sq. ft.; *Superheating surface* 930 sq. ft.; *Boiler diameter* 6 ft. 6 in.; *Coupled wheelbase* 12 ft. 10½ in. each engine; *Engine wheelbase* 31 ft. each engine; *Maximum axle load* 18.5 tons; *Adhesion weight* 109 tons; *Total engine weight* 211.5 tons; *Water capacity* 6,600 gal.; *Coal capacity* 10 tons; *Total wheelbase* 87 ft. 2 in.; *Total length over buffers* 96 ft. 7 in.

EGYPTIAN PASSENGER LOCOMOTIVES: Though the biggest Egyptian steam locomotives were Pacifics, the backbone of post-war motive power was heavy 4–6–0s in two or three classes. But a beginning with main-line diesel traction was made in 1957 and within 10 years all the steam locomotives had been eliminated.

DATA: *Railway* Egyptian State; *Wheel arrangement* 4–6–0; *Type or class* E.10; *Builder* North British Loco. Co.; *Years built* 1950–51; *Cyl. (no.) bore and stroke* (2) 21 in. × 28 in.; *Driving wheel diameter* 6 ft.; *Boiler pressure* 225 lb.; *Tractive effort at 75% pressure* 29,000 lb.; *Total evap. surface* 2,191 sq. ft.; *Grate area* 31.2 sq. ft.; *Superheating surface* 420 sq. ft.; *Boiler diameter* 5 ft. 11 in.; *Coupled wheelbase* 16 ft.; *Engine wheelbase* 29 ft. 3 in.; *Maximum axle load* 21.1 tons; *Adhesion weight* 63 tons; *Total engine weight* 85.85 tons; *Water capacity* 5,500 gal.; *Coal capacity* 10 tons (oil); *Total wheelbase* 61 ft. 6 in. *Total length over buffers* 70 ft.; *Engine and tender weight* 154.65 tons.

LIGHT MIKADOS IN KENYA: Operation of the E.A.R. was so much associated with large Beyer-Garratt articulated locomotives that little notice was taken of the well-designed secondary-line engines, mainly 2–8–2 types, with 13-ton axle loads, beginning in the 1920s and ending with the 29-class in 1950.

DATA: *Railway* East African; *Wheel arrangement* 2–8–2; *Type or class* 29; *Builder* North British Loco. Co.; *Years built* 1950–51; *Cyl. (no.) bore and stroke* (2) 18 in. × 26 in.; *Driving wheel diameter* 4 ft.; *Boiler pressure* 200 lb.; *Tractive effort at 75% pressure* 26,350 lb.; *Total evap. surface* 1,878 sq. ft.; *Grate area* 38 sq. ft.; *Superheating surface* 446 sq. ft.; *Boiler diameter* 5 ft. 3 in.; *Coupled wheelbase* 13 ft. 3 in.; *Engine wheelbase* 30 ft. 5 in.; *Maximum axle load* 13 tons; *Adhesion weight* 51.9 tons; *Total engine weight* 73.8 tons; *Water capacity* 4,000 gal.; *Coal capacity* 2,375 gal. (oil); *Total wheelbase* 57 ft. 2 in.; *Total length over buffers* 65 ft. 3 in.; *Engine and tender weight* 126.3 tons.

3 FT. 6 IN. GAUGE GOODS ENGINE, GHANA: Engines of "Mountain" wheel arrangement were built over many years for the principal goods trains on the railway of Ghana and its predecessor, the Gold Coast Railway. Some had three cylinders, but after World War II only two-cylinder models were built.

DATA: *Railway* Ghana; *Wheel arrangement* 4–8–2; *Type or class* 221/130; *Builder* Vulcan Foundry; *Years built* 1947–48; *Cyl. (no.) bore and stroke* (2) $19\frac{1}{4}$ in. × 24 in.; *Driving wheel diameter* 3 ft. 9 in.; *Boiler pressure* 180 lb.; *Tractive effort at 75% pressure* 26,700 lb.; *Total evap. surface* 1,973 sq. ft.; *Grate area* 32 sq. ft.; *Superheating surface* 347 sq. ft.; *Boiler diameter* 5 ft. 5 in.; *Coupled wheelbase* 12 ft. 9 in.; *Engine wheelbase* 30 ft. 9 in.; *Maximum axle load* 13.2 tons; *Adhesion weight* 52 tons; *Total engine weight* 74.2 tons; *Water capacity* 4,000 gal.; *Coal capacity* 8 tons; *Total wheelbase* 57 ft. $5\frac{1}{4}$ in.; *Total length over buffers* 65 ft. $7\frac{1}{2}$ in.; *Engine and tender weight* 118.8 tons.

SOUTH AFRICAN MOUNTAIN ENGINES: From 1909 the 4–8–2, or Mountain type, engines grew ever greater in size and power, reaching the peak in the immense 15F class, making full use of the wide loading gauge and heaviest rails. Many were built by British and European manufacturers. 3 ft. 6 in. rail gauge.

DATA: *Railway* South African; *Wheel arrangement* 4–8–2; *Type or class* 15F; *Builder* North British Loco. Co. and others; *Years built* 1945–46, etc.; *Cyl. (no.) bore and stroke* (2) 24 in. × 28 in.; *Driving wheel diameter* 5 ft.; *Boiler pressure* 210 lb. *Tractive effort at 75% pressure* 42,335 lb.; *Total evap. surface* 3,415 sq. ft.; *Grate area* 62.5 sq. ft.; *Superheating surface* 661 sq. ft.; *Boiler diameter* 6 ft. 7½ in.; *Coupled wheelbase* 15 ft. 9 in.; *Engine wheelbase* 35 ft. 8 in.; *Maximum axle load* 18.1 tons; *Adhesion weight* 71.9 tons; *Total engine weight* 111.6 tons; *Water capacity* 6,050 gal.; *Coal capacity* 14 tons; *Total wheelbase* 65 ft. 6¼ in.; *Total length over buffers* 74 ft.; *Engine and tender weight* 181 tons.

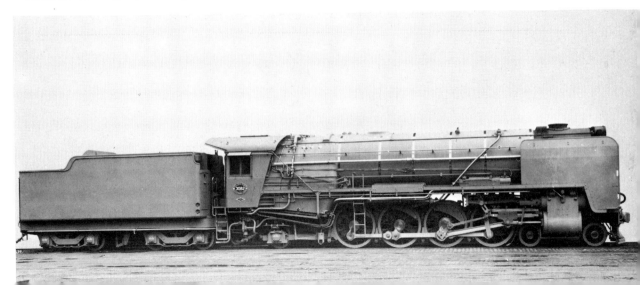

LIGHT EIGHT-COUPLED ENGINES, SOUTH AFRICA: In contradistinction to the big 15F Mountain engines, the 24-class 2–8–4s were built to give great power on an axle load of only 11¼ tons, 38 per cent less than in the 15F. They have comparatively big tenders for the engine size, to suit long-time through runs. 3 ft. 6 in. rail gauge.

DATA: *Railway* South African; *Wheel arrangement* 2–8–4; *Type or class* 24; *Builder* North British Loco. Co.; *Year built* 1950; *Cyl. (no.) bore and stroke* (2) 19 in. × 26 in.; *Driving wheel diameter* 4 ft. 3 in.; *Boiler pressure* 200 lb.; *Tractive effort at 75% pressure* 27,600 lb.; *Total evap. surface* 1,641 sq. ft.; *Grate area* 36 sq. ft.; *Superheating surface* 380 sq. ft.; *Boiler diameter* 5 ft. 3 in.; *Coupled wheelbase* 13 ft. 6 in.; *Engine wheelbase* 31 ft.; *Maximum axle load* 11.2 tons; *Adhesion weight* 43.9 tons; *Total engine weight* 70.85 tons; *Water capacity* 4,500 gal.; *Coal capacity* 9 tons; *Total wheelbase* 65 ft. 3½ in.; *Total length over buffers* 75 ft. 4 in.; *Engine and tender weight* 127 tons.

CONDENSING ENGINES IN SOUTH AFRICA: These enormous machines formed the culmination of the steam locomotive in South Africa. Half of them had ordinary high-capacity tenders; the other half had huge Henschel condensing tenders so that the engines could run 600 miles without re-watering, and so avoid the bad-water points. 3 ft. 6 in. rail gauge.

DATA: *Railway* South African; *Wheel arrangement* 4—8—4; *Type or class* 25 NC; *Builder* NBL and Henschel; *Years built* 1953-54; *Cyl. (no.) bore and stroke* (2) 24 in. × 28 in.; *Driving wheel diameter* 5 ft.; *Boiler pressure* 225 lb.; *Tractive effort at 75% pressure* 43,800 lb.; *Total evap. surface* 3,390 sq. ft.; *Grate area* 70 sq. ft.; *Superheating surface* 600 sq. ft.; *Boiler diameter* 6 ft. 4 in.; *Coupled wheelbase* 15 ft. 9 in.; *Engine wheelbase* 37 ft. 9 in.; *Maximum axle load* 18.8 tons; *Adhesion weight* 75 tons; *Total engine weight* 119 tons; *Water capacity* 10,500 gal.; *Coal capacity* 18 tons; *Total wheelbase* 81 ft. 1¾ in.; *Total length over buffers* 91 ft. 9½ in.; *Engine and tender weight* 227 tons.

EARLY INDIAN STANDARD FREIGHT CLASS: This was the third Indian "standard" locomotive, to a design approved by the British Engineering Standards Association (BESA) in 1902 as suitable for heavy freight haulage on most Indian broad-gauge (5 ft. 6 in.) railways. It was built in hundreds until new standards were evolved in 1926–27.

DATA: *Railway* Indian State, Bengal-Nagpur, etc.; *Wheel arrangement* 2–8–0; *Type or class* BESA Standard; *Builder* Robt. Stephenson, Vulcan, etc.; *Years built* 1903–25; *Cyl. (no.) bore and stroke* (2) 21 in. × 26 in.; *Driving wheel diameter* 4 ft. 8½ in.; *Boiler pressure* 180 lb.; *Tractive effort at 75% pressure* 27,400 lb.; *Total evap. surface* 2,087 sq. ft.; *Grate area* 332 sq. ft.; *Superheating surface* Nil originally; 226 sq. ft. later; *Boiler diameter* 5 ft. 6 in.; *Coupled wheelbase* 16 ft.; *Engine wheelbase* 25 ft.; *Maximum axle load* 16 tons; *Adhesion weight* 63.75 tons; *Total engine weight* 71.25 tons; *Water capacity* 4,000 gal.; *Coal capacity* 7 tons; *Total wheelbase* 50 ft. 4½ in.; *Total length over buffers* 60 ft. 3⅞ in.; *Engine and tender weight* 118 tons.

G.I.P. FOUR-CYLINDER DECAPODS: These huge engines, with 7 ft. diameter over the boiler lagging, were built to haul goods trains up the 1 in 37 Ghat incline inland from Bombay and then on to Igatpuri. They were oil-burners, and after the Ghat line was electrified they were transferred to the old Indian North Western Railway (now the Pakistan Western Railway). 5 ft. 6 in. rail gauge.

DATA: *Railway* Great Indian Peninsula; *Wheel arrangement* 2–10–0; *Type or class* N/1; *Builder* North British Loco. Co.; *Year built* 1921; *Cyl. (no.) bore and stroke* (4) 20 in. × 26 in.; *Driving wheel diameter* 4 ft. 8½ in.; *Boiler pressure* 160 lb.; *Tractive effort at 75% pressure* 44,175 lb.; *Total evap. surface* 2,968 sq. ft.; *Grate area* 44 sq. ft.; *Superheating surface* 617 sq. ft.; *Boiler diameter* 6 ft. 6¾ in.; *Coupled wheelbase* 22 ft. 0¾ in.; *Engine wheelbase* 31 ft. 3¾ in.; *Maximum axle load* 19 tons; *Adhesion weight* 95 tons; *Total engine weight* 108 tons; *Water capacity* 5,000 gal.; *Fuel capacity* 9 tons (oil; or 12 tons coal); *Total wheelbase* 61 ft. 1¾ in.; *Total length over buffers* 70 ft. 5 in.; *Engine and tender weight* 174.5 tons.

METRE-GAUGE HEAVY GOODS ENGINES, INDIA: In the 1920s, three large groups of standard engines were evolved in India. Those for the 5 ft. 6 in. gauge were classed X; those for metre-gauge Y, and those for 2 ft. 6 in. gauge Z. The principal types for metre-gauge were the YB Pacific, and YD Mikado shown here.

DATA: *Railway* Indian State; Burma State; *Wheel arrangement* 2–8–2; *Type or class* YD; *Builder* Vulcan; Nasmyth; etc.; *Years built* 1927–48; *Cyl. (no.) bore and stroke* (2) 17 in. × 24 in.; *Driving wheel diameter* 4 ft.; *Boiler pressure* 180 lb.; *Tractive effort at 75% pressure* 19,450 lb.; *Total evap. surface* 1,391 sq. ft.; *Grate area* 26 sq. ft.; *Superheating surface* 310 sq. ft.; *Boiler diameter* 4 ft. 11½ in.; *Coupled wheelbase* 13 ft. 5 in.; *Engine wheelbase* 27 ft. 9 in.; *Maximum axle load* 10 tons; *Adhesion weight* 39.65 tons; *Total engine weight* 56.6 tons; *Water capacity* 3,000 gal.; *Coal capacity* 4.5 tons; *Total wheelbase* 50 ft. 5 in.; *Total length over buffers* 60 ft. 1 in.; *Engine and tender weight* 93 tons.

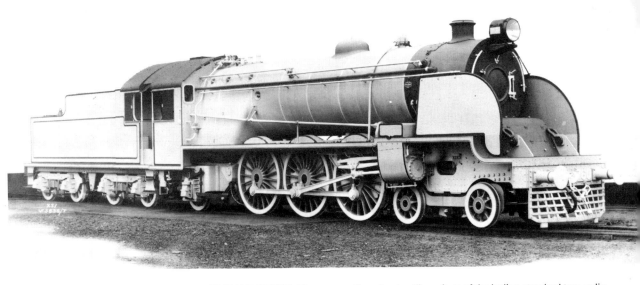

FOUR-CYLINDER POPPET-VALVE INDIAN PACIFIC: These were "modernised" versions of the Indian standard two-cylinder XC-class Pacifics, built to test out multi-cylinder propulsion and poppet valves against two cylinders with piston valves and Walschaerts motion. Only four were built. 5 ft. 6 in. rail gauge.

DATA: *Railway* Indian State; *Wheel arrangement* 4–6–2; *Type or class* XS1 and XS2; *Builder* Vulcan Foundry; *Year built* 1930; *Cyl (no.) bore and stroke* (4) 16 in. × 26 in.; *Driving wheel diameter* 6 ft. 2 in.; *Boiler pressure* 225 lb.; *Tractive effort at* 75% *pressure* 30,400 lb.; *Total evap. surface* 2,397 sq. ft.; *Grate area* 51 sq. ft.; *Superheating surface* 688 sq. ft.; *Boiler diameter* 6 ft. 3 in.; *Coupled wheelbase* 13 ft. 2 in.; *Engine wheelbase* 35 ft. 5 in.; *Maximum axle load* 21.5 tons; *Adhesion weight* 64.5 tons; *Total engine weight* 108 tons; *Water capacity* 4,500 gal.; *Coal capacity* 10 tons; *Total wheelbase* 67 ft. 2 in.; *Total length over buffers* 79 ft. 5 in.; *Engine and tender weight* 172.2 tons.

CHINESE LIGHT-LINE ENGINE: A good example from the years 1920–35 of a simple light weight engine for up-country lines where there was little skilled maintenance. There was grease lubrication in place of oil. Two centre couplers at each end to suit different wagons.

DATA: *Railway* Hangchow-Kiangshan (China); *Wheel arrangement* 4–8–0; *Type or class* 405; *Builder* Hunslet Engine Co.; *Year built* 1933; *Cyl. (no.) bore and stroke* (2) 16.25 in. × 21.6 in.; *Driving wheel diameter* 3 ft. 8 in.; *Boiler pressure* 200 lb.; *Tractive effort at 75% pressure* 19,500 lb.; *Total evap. surface* 871 sq. ft.; *Grate area* 19.4 sq. ft.; *Superheating surface* 376 sq. ft.; *Boiler diameter* 4 ft.; *Coupled wheelbase* 12 ft. $9\frac{3}{4}$ in.; *Engine wheelbase* 22 ft. $0\frac{1}{4}$ in.; *Maximum axle load* 8.25 tons; *Adhesion weight* 32.7 tons; *Total engine weight* 44.9 tons; *Water capacity* 2,640 gal.; *Coal capacity* 4 tons; *Total wheelbase* 45 ft. $3\frac{5}{8}$ in.; *Total length over buffers* 54 ft. $8\frac{3}{4}$ in.; *Engine and tender weight* 76.5 tons.

FOUR-AXLE COAL ENGINE, CHINA: A plain and simple engine for light rails and bridges but with all the fittings and proportions of the last stage in steam locomotive construction. Compared with the boiler size the grate was large, to burn low-quality coal with much ash.

DATA: *Railway* King Kan, China; *Wheel arrangement* 0–8–0; *Type or class* 3; *Builder* North British Loco. Co.; *Years built* 1949–50; *Cyl. (no.) bore and stroke* (2) 16.6 in. × 23.6 in.; *Driving wheel diameter* 3 ft. 11¼ in.; *Boiler pressure* 213 lb.; *Tractive effort at 75% pressure* 21,900 lb.; *Total evap. surface* 1,120 sq. ft.; *Grate area* 32.3 sq. ft.; *Superheating surface* 439 sq. ft.; *Boiler diameter* 4 ft. 9 in.; *Coupled wheelbase* 16 ft. 3 in.; *Engine wheelbase* 16 ft. 3 in.; *Maximum axle load* 13.5 tons; *Adhesion weight* 52.8 tons; *Total engine weight* 52.8 tons; *Water capacity* 3,300 gal.; *Coal capacity* 10 tons; *Total wheelbase* 45 ft. 8¾ in.; *Total length over buffers* 59 ft.; *Engine and tender weight* 94.6 tons.

SOUTH AUSTRALIAN MOUNTAIN ENGINES: These were the largest non-articulated engines ever built in Britain. They had bar frames and were almost entirely to American conceptions, and they began that Americanisation of Australian motive power that is still evident today. After a few years they were rebuilt into 4–8–4s.

DATA: *Railway* South Australian; *Wheel arrangement* 4–8–2; *Type or class* 500; *Builder* Armstrong Whitworth; *Years built* 1925–26; *Cyl. (no.) bore and stroke* (2) 26 in. × 28 in.; *Driving wheel diameter* 5 ft. 3 in.; *Boiler pressure* 200 lb.; *Tractive effort at 75% pressure* 45,000 lb.; *Total evap. surface* 3,609 sq. ft.; *Grate area* 66.6 sq. ft.; *Superheating surface* 835 sq. ft.; *Boiler diameter* 7 ft. 0½ in./6 ft. 2 in. taper; *Coupled wheelbase* 17 ft.; *Engine wheelbase* 39 ft. 2 in.; *Maximum axle load* 22.8 tons; *Adhesion weight* 89 tons; *Total engine weight* 134.9 tons; *Water capacity* 8,000 gal.; *Coal capacity* 12 tons; *Total wheelbase* 73 ft. 11 in.; *Total length over buffers* 82 ft. 6 in.; *Engine and tender weight* 218.8 tons.

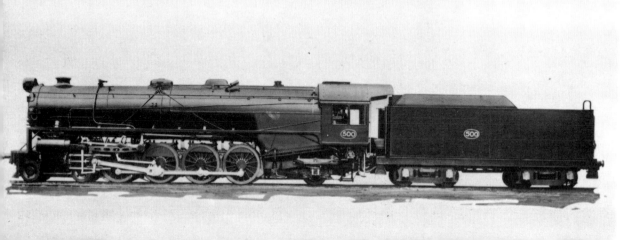

BRITISH-BUILT 4–6–4 TYPE FOR VICTORIA: The last and not the most successful steam power built for the Victorian Railways. They had roller-bearing axleboxes and many modern fittings; but they had several troubles, and by the time they were completed they were not welcome, as a diesel policy had then been decided.

DATA: *Railway* Victorian; *Wheel arrangement* 4–6–4; *Type or class* R; *Builder* North British Loco.; *Year built* 1951; *Cyl. (no.) bore and stroke* (2) 21.5 in. × 28 in.; *Driving wheel diameter* 6 ft. 1 in.; *Boiler pressure* 210 lb.; *Tractive effort at 75% pressure* 28,000 lb.; *Total evap. surface* 2,243 sq. ft.; *Grate area* 42 sq. ft.; *Superheating surface* 462 sq. ft.; *Boiler diameter* 6 ft./5 ft. 7 in. taper; *Coupled wheelbase* 12 ft. 10 in.; *Engine wheelbase* 36 ft. 3 in.; *Maximum axle load* 19.6 tons; *Adhesion weight* 58.5 tons; *Total engine weight* 107.6 tons; *Water capacity* 9,000 gal.; *Coal capacity* 6 tons; *Total wheelbase* 67 ft.; *Total length over buffers* 77 ft. 3½ in.; *Engine and tender weight* 186.4 tons.

123

LARGE GENERAL-PURPOSE ENGINES IN NEW ZEALAND: Many fine 4–8–4 engines were constructed in New Zealand and Glasgow over a period of 20 years for the N.Z.G.R., and their great relative power was obtained despite the diminutive loading gauge of 11 ft. 3 in. height and 8 ft. 6 in. wide, allied to the narrow rail gauge of 3 ft. 6 in.

DATA: *Railway* New Zealand Government; *Wheel arrangement* 4–8–4; *Type or class* K, Ka, Kb; *Builder* Railway, Hutt Valley; NBL; *Years built* 1931–50; *Cyl. (no.) bore and stroke* (2) 20.5 in. × 26 in.; *Driving wheel diameter* 4 ft. 6 in.; *Boiler pressure* 200 lb.; *Tractive effort at 75% pressure* 30,350 lb. + 6,000 lb. booster; *Total evap. surface* 1,935 sq. ft.; *Grate area* 47.7 sq. ft.; *Superheating surface* 428 sq. ft.; *Boiler diameter* 5 ft. 6 in.; *Coupled wheelbase* 14 ft. 3 in.; *Engine wheelbase* 34 ft. 10 in.; *Maximum axle load* 13.5 tons; *Adhesion weight* 52.5 tons + 13 tons for booster; *Total engine weight* 94.5 tons; *Water capacity* 5,000 gal.; *Coal capacity* 7.5 tons; *Total wheelbase* 61 ft. 7 in.; *Total length over buffers* 69 ft. 11 in.; *Engine and tender weight* 142.5 tons.

EXPRESS ARTICULATED LOCOMOTIVE IN BRAZIL: After a couple of Tasmanian engines in 1912, this was the first express passenger Beyer Garratt. After some five years of service the engines were rebuilt as 4–6–2 + 2–6–4, which gave steadier riding and increased the possible water capacity. They run on the unusual gauge of 5 ft. 3 in.

DATA: *Railway* San Paulo, Brazil; *Wheel arrangement* 2–6–2 + 2–6–2; *Type or class* 163; *Builder* Beyer Peacock; *Years built* 1926–27; *Cyl. (no.) bore and stroke* (4) 20 in. × 26 in.; *Driving wheel diameter* 5 ft. 6 in.; *Boiler pressure* 200 lb.; *Tractive effort at 75% pressure* 47,250 lb.; *Total evap. surface* 2,954 sq. ft.; *Grate area* 49.2 sq. ft.; *Superheating surface* 668 sq. ft.; *Boiler diameter* 6 ft. 10 in.; *Coupled wheelbase* 12 ft. each engine; *Engine wheelbase* 25 ft. 7 in. each engine; *Maximum axle load* 18.5 tons; *Adhesion weight* 111 tons; *Total engine weight* 158.25 tons; *Water capacity* 3,100 gal.; *Coal capacity* 5 tons; *Total wheelbase* 73 ft.; *Total length over buffers* 81 ft. 6 in.

ADHESION ENGINES FOR STEEP GRADIENTS, COLOMBIA: These engines were an attempt to modernise Colombian motive power in the 1920s, by combining the best features of English and American practice and giving the contracts to European builders. The gauge was very narrow (3 ft.), and the engines had to work up long grades of 1 in 20 to 25.
DATA: *Railway* Colombian National (Pacific); *Wheel arrangement* 4–6–2; *Type or class* 48; *Builder* Schwartzkopff; *Year built* 1927; *Cyl. (no.) bore and stroke* (3) 16 in. × 20 in.; *Driving wheel diameter* 4 ft. 2 in.; *Boiler pressure* 180 lb.; *Tractive effort at 75% pressure* 20,730 lb.; *Total evap. surface* 1,323 sq. ft.; *Grate area* 30.2 sq. ft.; *Superheating surface* 330 sq. ft.; *Boiler diameter* 4 ft. 9 in.; *Coupled wheelbase* 9 ft. 6 in.; *Engine wheelbase* 26 ft. 1 in.; *Maximum axle load* 12.2 tons; *Adhesion weight* 35.9 tons; *Total engine weight* 56.5 tons; *Water capacity* 2,750 gal.; *Coal capacity* 5.25 tons; *Total wheelbase* 49 ft. 7½ in.; *Total length over buffers* 57 ft. 0½ in.; *Engine and tender weight* 87.5 tons.

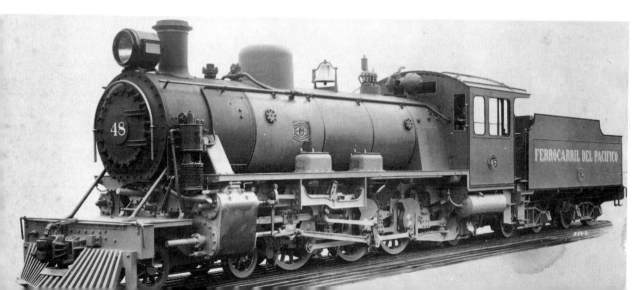

SUBURBAN COMPOUND TANKS, BUENOS AIRES: For a suburban engine making frequent starts this was a peculiar design for it was two-cylinder compound. The Central Argentine main-line engines of the time, 4–6–2 and 2–8–2, were also two-cylinder compounds; but in 1930 a change was made to three-cylinder simple-expansion Pacifics. 5 ft. 6 in. rail gauge.

DATA: *Railway* Central Argentine; *Wheel arrangement* 4–8–4T; *Type or class* 500; *Builder* Armstrong-Whitworth; *Year built* 1928; *Cyl. (no.) bore and stroke* (1) 22.5 in. × 26 in. h.p. (1) 31.5 in. × 26 in. l.p.; *Driving wheel diameter* 5 ft. 2 in.; *Boiler pressure* 200 lb.; *Tractive effort at 75% pressure* 25,000 lb.; *Total evap. surface* 1,602 sq. ft.; *Grate area* 27 sq. ft.; *Super-heating surface* 277 sq. ft.; *Boiler diameter* 5 ft. 9 in.; *Coupled wheelbase* 16 ft. 6 in.; *Engine wheelbase* 39 ft. 10 in.; *Maximum axle load* 16 tons; *Adhesion weight* 63 tons; *Total engine weight* 110 tons; *Water capacity* 2,500 gal.; *Coal capacity* 3.5 tons; *Total wheelbase* —; *Total length over buffers* 51 ft. 7 in.

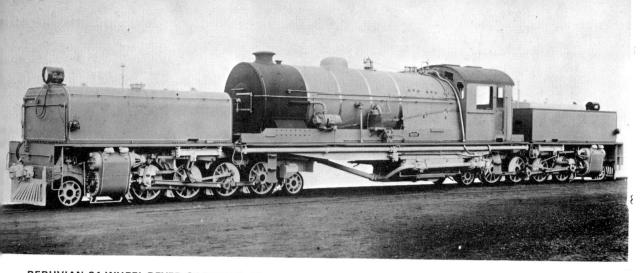

PERUVIAN 24-WHEEL BEYER-GARRATTS: These oil-burners on the highest standard-gauge railway in the world reached the summit of 15,806 ft. in 107 miles from Callao docks through 61 tunnels and 13 V-reversing stations by means of long 1 in 22 to 25 gradients. They were the first English-built locomotives to have 7-ft. boilers.

DATA: *Railway* Central of Peru; *Wheel arrangement* 2–8–2 + 2–8–2; *Type or class* 125; *Builder* Beyer Peacock; *Year built* 1930; *Cyl. (no.) bore and stroke* (4) 19.5 in. × 22 in.; *Driving wheel diameter* 3 ft. 9 in.; *Boiler pressure* 205 lb.; *Tractive effort at 75% pressure* 57,150 lb.; *Total evap. surface* 2,842 sq. ft.; *Grate area* 61.2 sq. ft.; *Superheating surface* 678 sq. ft.; *Boiler diameter* 7 ft. 3½ in.; *Coupled wheelbase* 12 ft. 6 in. each engine; *Engine wheelbase* 23 ft. 9 in. each engine; *Maximum axle load* 16.5 tons; *Adhesion weight* 131.5 tons; *Total engine weight* 181 tons; *Water capacity* 5,300 gal.; *Coal capacity* 1,550 gal. of oil; *Total wheelbase* 72 ft. 4 in.; *Total length over buffers* 80 ft. 2 in.

THE PENNSYLVANIA PACIFICS: These 425 locomotives were among the most famous Pacifics ever built and maintained the Pennsylvania's fastest passenger trains for over 20 years from 1918 on the east and west divisions flanking the central Allegheny mountain division.

DATA: *Railway* Pennsylvania; *Wheel arrangement* 4–6–2; *Type or class* K4S; *Builder* Railway, at Altoona; Baldwin; *Years built* 1914–27; *Cyl. (no.) bore and stroke* (2) 27 in. × 28 in; *Driving wheel diameter* 6 ft. 8 in.; *Boiler pressure* 205 lb.; *Tractive effort at 75% pressure* 39,300 lb.; *Total evap. surface* 4,028; *Grate area* 70 sq. ft.; *Superheating surface* 1,215 sq. ft.; *Boiler diameter* 7 ft. 5 in./6 ft. 5 in. taper; *Coupled wheelbase* 13 ft. 10 in.; *Engine wheelbase* 36 ft. 2 in.; *Maximum axle load* 30 tons; *Adhesion weight* 90 tons; *Total engine weight* 138 tons; *Water capacity* 5,800 gal.; *Coal capacity* 11.6 tons; *Total wheelbase* 72 ft. 4 in.; *Total length over buffers* 80 ft. 5½ in.

TEXAN 2–10–4, U.S.A.: In 1924 a big advance in the power of American locomotives began by putting a four-wheel truck under the cab in place of a single axle. This enabled much bigger fireboxes to be carried. First of the new idea were 2–8–4s, but the 2–10–4s followed almost at once.

DATA: *Railway* Texas & Pacific; *Wheel arrangement* 2–10–4; *Type or class* 660; *Builder* Lima; *Year built* 1925; *Cyl. (no.) bore and stroke* (2) 29 in. × 32 in.; *Driving wheel diameter* 5 ft. 3 in.; *Boiler pressure* 255 lb.; *Tractive effort at 75% pressure* 97,900 lb. with booster; *Total evap. surface* 5,113 sq. ft.; *Grate area* 100 sq. ft.; *Superheating surface* 2,100 sq. ft.; *Boiler diameter* 7 ft. 2½ in.; *Coupled wheelbase* 22 ft.; *Engine wheelbase* 46 ft. 8 in.; *Maximum axle load* 27.7 tons; *Adhesion weight* 137 tons + 19.4 tons for booster; *Total engine weight* 204 tons; *Water capacity* 10,650 gal.; *Fuel capacity* 4,175 gal. of oil; *Total wheelbase* 86 ft. 8 in.; *Total length over buffers* 97 ft.; *Engine and tender weight* 329 tons.

AMERICAN 0–8–0 STEAM SWITCHER: Because of the very heavy freight trains, shunting engines in North America were of vast size. This wide-firebox comparatively clean-looking type had nearly 120 tons of adhesion weight, and an immense tender, so that yard work was not hindered by frequent visits to the water column.

DATA: *Railway* Delaware & Hudson; *Wheel arrangement* 0–8–0; *Type or class* B-7; *Builder* Alco; *Years built* 1906–08 (completely modernised 1926–30); *Cyl. (no.) bore and stroke* (2) 25.5 in. × 30 in.; *Driving wheel diameter* 4 ft. 9 in.; *Boiler pressure* 225 lb.; *Tractive effort at 75% pressure* 58,000 lb; *Total evap. surface* 3,160 sq. ft.; *Grate area* 86 sq. ft.; *Superheating surface* 671 sq. ft.; *Boiler diameter* 6 ft. 10 in.; *Coupled wheelbase* 17 ft.; *Engine wheelbase* 17 ft.; *Maximum axle load* 30 tons; *Adhesion weight* 118.5 tons; *Total engine weight* 118.5 tons; *Water capacity* 7,500 gal.; *Coal capacity* 12.5 tons; *Total wheelbase* 56 ft. 8½ in.; *Total length over buffers* 73 ft. 9⅞ in.; *Engine and tender weight* 178 tons.

131

NEW YORK CENTRAL HUDSONS: Among the world's most remarkable express passenger locomotives. They could be worked long distances at 60/65 m.p.h. with full regulator and 60/65 per cent cut-off, and could haul 1,000-ton trains along the level at 75 m.p.h. There were 275 of them on the N.Y.C.

DATA: *Railway* New York Central; *Wheel arrangement* 4–6–4 (Hudson); *Type or class* J-Ie; *Builder* Alco; *Years built* 1927–31; *Cyl. (no.) bore and stroke* (2) 25 in. × 28 in.; *Driving wheel diameter* 6 ft. 7 in.; *Boiler pressure* 225 lb.; *Tractive effort at 75% pressure* 37,500 lb.; *Total evap. surface* 4,484 sq. ft.; *Grate area* 81.5 sq. ft.; *Superheating surface* 1,951 sq. ft.; *Boiler diameter* 6 ft. 10½ in.; *Coupled wheelbase* 14 ft.; *Engine wheelbase* 40 ft. 4 in.; *Maximum axle load* 28.4 tons; *Adhesion weight* 84.9 tons; *Total engine weight* 159 tons; *Water capacity* 12,500 gal.; *Coal capacity* 21.4 tons; *Total wheelbase* 83 ft. 8 in.; *Total length over buffers* 96 ft.; *Engine and tender weight* 297 tons.

CANADA'S LARGEST STEAM PASSENGER ENGINES: At a time when big eight-coupled passenger engines were coming into vogue in North America, the C.N.R. was a leader with the immense 6100 class, the largest steam passenger engines ever to run in the Dominion.

DATA: *Railway* Canadian National; *Wheel arrangement* 4–8–4; *Type or class* 6100; *Builder* Canadian Loco.; Montreal Loco.; *Years built* 1927–28; *Cyl. (no.) bore and stroke* (2) 25.5 in. × 30 in.; *Driving wheel diameter* 6 ft. 1 in.; *Boiler pressure* 250 lb.; *Tractive effort at 75% pressure* 50,100 lb.; *Total evap. surface* 4,256 sq. ft.; *Grate area* 84.4 sq. ft.; *Superheating surface* 1,700 sq. ft.; *Boiler diameter* 7 ft. 6 in./6 ft. 9 in. taper; *Coupled wheelbase* 19 ft. 6 in.; *Engine wheelbase* 43 ft. 10 in.; *Maximum axle load* 26 tons; *Adhesion weight* 102.7 tons; *Total engine weight* 168.75 tons; *Water capacity* 11,300 gal.; *Coal capacity* 18 tons; *Total wheelbase* 82 ft.; *Total length over buffers* 94 ft. 6 in.; *Engine and tender weight* 284.75 tons.

U.P. 12-COUPLED FAST FREIGHTERS: These engines were the U.P.'s effort to work its fastest and heaviest freight trains without recourse to a Mallet articulated type. There were 88 of them, and they had an adhesion weight 50 per cent more than that of the next largest 12-coupled engine in the world.

DATA: *Railway* Union Pacific; *Wheel arrangement* 4–12–2; *Type or class* 9000; *Builder* Alco; *Years built* 1927–30; *Cyl. (no.) bore and stroke* (2) 27 in. × 32 in; (1) 27 in. × 31 in.; *Driving wheel diameter* 5 ft. 7 in.; *Boiler pressure* 220 lb.; *Tractive effort at 75% pressure* 85,000 lb.; *Total evap. surface* 5,853 sq. ft.; *Grate area* 108 sq. ft.; *Superheating surface* 2,580 sq. ft.; *Boiler diameter* 7 ft. 6 in.; *Coupled wheelbase* 30 ft. 8 in.; *Engine wheelbase* 52 ft. 4 in.; *Maximum axle load* 26.7 tons; *Adhesion weight* 159 tons; *Total engine weight* 222 tons; *Water capacity* 15,000 gal.; *Coal capacity* 19.7 tons; *Total wheelbase* 91 ft. 6½ in.; *Total length over buffers* 102 ft.; *Engine and tender weight* 361 tons.

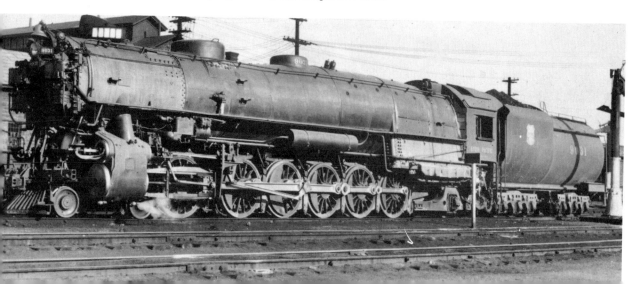

MALLET ARTICULATED ENGINE, U.S.A.: A typical example of the last era in the construction of enormous Mallet articulated locomotives; with wheels big enough, and valve gear adequate, for passenger train speeds, and yet equally suited to fast freight haulage.

DATA: *Railway* Pittsburgh & West Virginia; *Wheel arrangement* 2–6–6–4; *Type or class* 1101; *Builder* Baldwin; *Year built* 1935; *Cyl. (no.) bore and stroke* (4) 23 in. × 32. in.; *Driving wheel diameter* 5 ft. 3 in.; *Boiler pressure* 225 lb.; *Tractive effort at 75% pressure* 89,000 lb.; *Total evap. surface* 5,913 sq. ft.; *Grate area* 102.3 sq. ft.; *Superheating surface* 1,873 sq. ft.; *Boiler diameter* 7 ft. 10 in.; *Coupled wheelbase* 11 ft. each group; *Engine wheelbase* 55 ft. 8 in.; *Maximum axle load* 30 tons; *Adhesion weight* 177.2 tons; *Total engine weight* 235.5 tons; *Water capacity* 16,600 gal.; *Coal capacity* 17.8 tons; *Total wheelbase* 98 ft. 4 in.; *Total length over buffers* 108 ft.; *Engine and tender weight* 404 tons.

HIAWATHA STREAMLINED ATLANTICS: The last, the largest, and the fastest Atlantics ever built. They *did*, attain 100 m.p.h. almost every working day on the streamlined Hiawatha train between Chicago and the Twin Cities from 1935 until after the entry of the U.S.A. into the World War II.

DATA: *Railway* Chicago, Milwaukee, St. Paul & Pacific; *Wheel arrangement* 4—4—2; *Type or class* No. 1; *Builder* Alco; *Years built* 1934—35; *Cyl. (no.) bore and stroke* (2) 19 in. × 28 in.; *Driving wheel diameter* 7 ft.; *Boiler pressure* 300 lb.; *Tractive effort at 75% pressure* 27,200 lb.; *Total evap. surface* 3,245 sq. ft.; *Grate area* 69 sq. ft.; *Superheating surface* 1,029 sq. ft.; *Boiler diameter* 6 ft. 8 in./6 ft. 4¾ in. taper; *Coupled wheelbase* 8 ft. 6 in.; *Engine wheelbase* 37 ft. 7 in.; *Maximum axle load* 31.5 tons; *Adhesion weight* 62.5 tons; *Total engine weight* 125.5 tons; *Water capacity* 10,850 gal.; *Fuel capacity* 3,350 gal. (oil); *Total wheelbase* 78 ft. 10½ in.; *Total length over buffers* 88 ft. 8 in.; *Engine and tender weight* 236 tons.

FAST-FREIGHT MALLETS, UNION PACIFIC: Though not the biggest of Mallets (which were the 535-ton 4–8–8–4 Big Boy class of the U.P.) these 4–6–6–4 Challenger-class engines operated both express passenger and express freight trains over difficult divisions. Judged by American standards their tenders were not big.

DATA: *Railway* Union Pacific; *Wheel arrangement* 4–6–6–4; *Type or class* 3900; *Builder* Alco; *Year built* 1936; *Cyl. (no.) bore and stroke* (4) 22 in. × 32 in.; *Driving wheel diameter* 5 ft. 9 in.; *Boiler pressure* 255 lb.; *Tractive effort at 75% pressure* 86,000 lb.; *Total evap. surface* 5,381 sq. ft.; *Grate area* 108.2 sq. ft.; *Superheating surface* 1,650 sq. ft.; *Boiler diameter* 8 ft. 2 in.; *Coupled wheelbase* 12 ft. 2 in. each group; *Engine wheelbase* 59 ft. 11 in.; *Maximum axle load* 29 tons; *Adhesion weight* 172.5 tons; *Total engine weight* 253 tons; *Water capacity* 15,300 gal.; *Coal capacity* 20 tons; *Total wheelbase* 97 ft. 10½ in.; *Total length over buffers* 107 ft. 9 in.; *Engine and tender weight* 391 tons.

A PENNSYLVANIA DUPLEX: About 75 locomotives with two sets of driving gear in one frame were built during World-War II years, of 4–4–4–4, 4–6–4–4, and 4–4–6–4 wheel arrangements. Though of great power, they were expensive near failures and had a short life.

DATA: *Railway* Pennsylvania; *Wheel arrangement* 4–4–6–4; *Type or class* Q-2; *Builder* Railway, at Altoona; *Years built* 1944–45; *Cyl. (no.) bore and stroke* (2) 19.75 in. × 28 in.; (2) 23.75 in. × 29 in.; *Driving wheel diameter* 5 ft. 9 in.; *Boiler pressure* 300 lb.; *Tractive effort at 75% pressure* 89,000 lb.; *Total evap. surface* 6,725 sq. ft.; *Grate area* 121.7 sq. ft.; *Superheating surface* 2,930 sq. ft.; *Boiler diameter* 8 ft. 2 in.; *Coupled wheelbase* 6 ft. 0½ in. one group; 12 ft. 1 in. second group; *Engine wheelbase* 53 ft. 5½ in.; *Maximum axle load* 35.5 tons; *Adhesion weight* 175.5 tons; *Total engine weight* 276 tons; *Water capacity* 15,900 gal.; *Coal capacity* 40 tons; *Total wheelbase* 107 ft. 7½ in.; *Total length over buffers* 124 ft. 7 in.; *Engine and tender weight* 469 tons.

DIESEL LOCOMOTIVES

The diesel engine used in locomotives is simply an enlarged version of a lorry engine, and like that engine it cannot start under load. Therefore a clutch and a transmission in one form or another must be inserted between the engine and the axles. In a lorry a gearbox and propeller shafting are enough; in a locomotive, because of the high h.p. and the heavy train weight, an electric or hydraulic system is necessary except in the smallest shunting locomotives. Single-unit diesel locomotives are now built up to 4,000 h.p., and in America up to 6,000 h.p.

The difference between petrol and diesel engines is that the former *sucks* in a mixture of petrol and air, which is compressed by the rising piston, and near the top of the stroke is fired by a spark from the magneto. In a diesel only air is compressed by the piston, and near top dead centre a high-pressure pump *forces* a small spray of oil into the cylinder; the air is so hot from its high compression that the oil spray is ignited immediately and forces the piston downward. The engine is kept cool by circulating water, which is itself cooled by big radiators cooled by fans. Little water is used, and the engine can run well over a thousand miles before rewatering. Both petrol and diesel engines have to be started without any load on them; only when they are running can the clutch be let in gently and the load applied. Electric and hydraulic systems act as both clutch and as a gearbox with an almost infinite number of steps.

In hydraulic systems one to three small oil turbines and fluid couplings are driven by the engine, and they change from one to the other automatically according to the tractive effort and speed. From them the power is taken through a reduction gear and cardan shafts to bevel gears on the axles. In the electric system a big generator or dynamo is driven by the engine, and the current produced by it is fed to several traction motors geared to the axles. In both cases the driver's control handle varies the amount of fuel injected into the engine, and so the power and r.p.m. For very heavy trains, two or three diesel locomotives can be coupled together and driven by one man, that is, in multiple.

THE DELTICS: The fastest and most powerful diesel locomotive class of British Railways, running often at 100 m.p.h. They are of light weight for their power, only 67 lb./h.p., and are confined to the East Coast Route express passenger services. The Deltic engine is a high-speed two-stroke opposed piston type of triangular form.

DATA: *Railway* British Railways; *Class or name* Deltic; *Type* d–e; *Axle arrangement* Co–Co; *Built by* English Electric; *Date built* 1961; *No. of engines and h.p.* 2 × 1650 = 3,300 b.h.p.; *Engine make* Napier; *Transmission make* English Electric; *Top speed* 100 m.p.h.; *Wheel diameter* 43 in.; *Bogie wheelbase* 13 ft. 6 in.; *Total wheelbase* 58 ft. 6 in.; *Maximum axle load* 16.5 tons; *Adhesion weight* 99 tons; *Total locomotive weight* 99 tons; *Fuel capacity* 900 gal.; *Continuous rated tractive effort and speed* 23,400 lb. at 45 m.p.h.; *Starting tractive effort* 50,000 lb.; *Train heating* boiler.

B.R. STANDARD TYPE 4 DIESEL-ELECTRICS: The standard diesel-electric main-line locomotive of British Railways. More than 500 have been built. Originally the engines were of 2,750 h.p., but had to be derated to 2,500 h.p. after numerous troubles. The oil engines are of heavy slow-speed vertical type with two crankshafts.

DATA: *Railway* British Railways; *Class or name* D.1500; *Type* d–e; *Axle arrangement* Co–Co; *Built by* Brush; *Dates built* 1961–66; *No. of engines and h.p.* 1 × 2,500 b.h.p.; *Engine make* Sulzer; *Transmission make* Brush; *Top speed* 90 m.p.h.; *Wheel diameter* 3 ft. 6 in.; *Bogie wheelbase* 14 ft. 6 in.; *Total wheelbase* 51 ft. 6 in.; *Maximum axle load* 19.5 tons; *Adhesion weight* 115 tons; *Total locomotive weight* 115 tons; *Fuel capacity* 800 gal.; *Continuous rated tractive effort and speed* 30,000 lb. at 27 m.p.h. *Starting tractive effort* 55,000 lb.; *Train heating* boiler.

B.R. 2,200 H.P. TYPE 4 DIESEL-HYDRAULICS: These were the original express diesel locomotives of the Western Region, but top-class services now are worked by the more powerful D.1000 class. In the first few years of modernization the Western Region had only hydraulic transmission, in conjunction with two high-speed engines for big locomotives.
DATA: *Railway* British Railways; *Class or name* D.800; *Type* d–h; *Axle arrangement* B–B; *Built by* Railway, at Swindon; *Dates built* 1958–61; *No. of engines and h.p.* 2 × 1,100 = 2,200 b.h.p.; *Engine make* Maybach and M.A.N.; *Transmission make* Mekydro and Voith; *Top speed* 90 m.p.h.; *Wheel diameter* 39.5 in.; *Bogie wheelbase* 10 ft. 6 in.; *Total wheelbase* 48 ft. 3 in.; *Maximum axle load* 20 tons; *Adhesion weight* 79 tons; *Total locomotive weight* 79 tons; *Fuel capacity* 800 gal.; *Continuous rated tractive effort and speed* 37,500 lb. at 12.5 m.p.h.; *Starting tractive effort* 48,000 lb.; *Train heating* boiler.

GERMAN 4,000 H.P. DIESEL-HYDRAULIC: This was one of the earliest 4,000 h.p. diesel locomotives; with two oil engine-transmission groups. It was not repeated in Germany because increasing electrification took all the hardest jobs for which such power was needed. Hydraulic transmission and quick-running lightweight engines.

DATA: *Railway* German Federal; *Class or name* V.320; *Type* d–h; *Axle arrangement* C–C; *Built by* Henschel; *Date built* 1962; *No. of engines and h.p.* 2 × 2,000 = 4,000 b.h.p.; *Engine make* Mercedes-Benz; *Transmission make* Voith; *Top speed* 100 m.p.h.; *Wheel diameter* 43.5 in.; *Bogie wheelbase* 14 ft. 3 in.; *Total wheelbase* 58 ft. 1½ in.; *Maximum axle load* 20–75 tons; *Adhesion weight* 120 tons; *Total locomotive weight* 120 tons; *Fuel capacity* 1,100 gal.; *Continuous rated tractive effort and speed* 62,500 lb. at 16.8 m.p.h.; *Starting tractive effort* 80,000 lb.; *Train heating* boiler.

SPANISH 4,000 H.P. FOUR-AXLE LOCOMOTIVE: The Spanish National Railways, known as RENFE, have 32 diesel-hydraulic locomotives in which 4,000 h.p. has been obtained with the use of only four axles. Each has two engine-transmission sets. They are specially for fast passenger and goods trains from Madrid to Barcelona, Valencia and Cartagena.
DATA: *Railway* Spanish National; *Class or name* D.4000; *Type* d–h; *Axle arrangement* B–B; *Built by* Krauss Maffei; *Dates built* 1966–67; *No. and h.p. of engines* 2 × 2,000 = 4,000 b.h.p.; *Engine make* Maybach; *Transmission make* Mekydro; *Top speed* 87 m.p.h.; *Wheel diameter* 40 in.; *Bogie wheelbase* 10 ft. 6 in.; *Total wheelbase* 53 ft. 4 in.; *Maximum axle load* 21.7 tons; *Adhesion weight* 86.5 tons; *Total locomotive weight* 86.5 tons; *Fuel capacity* 1,100 gal.; *Continuous rated tractive effort and speed* 56,000 lb. at 5.7 m.p.h.; *Starting tractive effort* 62,000 lb.; *Train heating* boiler wagon behind.

EGYPTIAN DIESEL-ELECTRIC FOR 500-MILE RUNS: These diesel-electrics, with American-type slow-speed two-stroke oil engines, work the long-distance ore trains of big double-bogie wagons from Aswan to Cairo. Four out of the six axles are driven, but all axles carry a heavy load, of above 20 tons. Similar locomotives with all axles driven have one 1,900 h.p. engine.
DATA: *Railway* Egyptian State; *Class or name* KK; *Type* d–e; *Axle arrangement* A1A–A1A; *Built by* Henschel; *Date built* 1957; *No. of engines and h.p.* 2 × 950 = 1,900 b.h.p.; *Engine make* G.M.; *Transmission make* E.M.D.; *Top speed* 65 m.p.h.; *Wheel diameter* 42 in.; *Bogie wheelbase* 13 ft. 1½ in.; *Total wheelbase* 57 ft. 5 in.; *Maximum axle load* 22 tons; *Adhesion weight* 88 tons; *Total locomotive weight* 128 tons; *Fuel capacity* 2,400 gal.; *Continuous rated tractive effort and speed* 44,000 lb. at 13 m.p.h.; *Starting tractive effort* 48,000 lb.; *Train heating* None.

STANDARD DIESEL-HYDRAULIC FOR TROPICAL COUNTRIES: This is an attempt to get a powerful standard locomotive that could be supplied to either one-metre or 3 ft. 6 in. gauges in many tropical or semi-tropical countries where only light axle loads are possible. One high-speed engine and one hydraulic transmission. Such locomotives are running in Angola, Congo, Indonesia, Thailand and Burma.

DATA: *Railway* Indonesia, Angola, etc.; *Class or name* LEU Standard; *Type* d–h; *Axle arrangement* B–B; *Built by* Krupp; Krauss-Maffei; *Dates built* 1965–70; *No of engines and h.p.* 1 × 1,500 b.h.p.; *Engine make* MMB; *Transmission make* Voith; *Top speed* 55 to 60 m.p.h.; *Wheel diameter* 36 in.; *Bogie wheelbase* 7 ft. 2 in.; *Total wheelbase* 27 ft.; *Maximum axle load* 13 tons to 14 tons; *Adhesion weight* 52 tons to 56 tons; *Total locomotive weight* 52 tons to 56 tons; *Fuel capacity* 440 gal.; *Continuous rated tractive effort and speed* 25,800 lb. at 11.8 m.p.h.; *Starting tractive effort* 37,000 lb.; *Train heating* None.

B.R. STANDARD DIESEL SHUNTER: Of antiquated appearance and poor look-out, this shunter design dates from 1934–36. About 1,370 have been built altogether, with various slow-speed oil engine makes, the English Electric type predominating. There are only two traction motors, and all three axles are coupled by side rods. Found in all Regions.

DATA: *Railway* British Railways; *Class or name* 350 STD; *Type* d-e; *Axle arrangement* C; *Built by* Railway; *Dates built* 1948–60; *No. of engines and h.p.* 1 × 350 b.h.p.; *Engine make* English Electric; *Transmission make* English Electric; *Top speed* 20 m.p.h.; *Wheel diameter* 4 ft. 6 in.; *Rigid wheelbase* 11 ft. 6 in.; *Total wheelbase* 11 ft. 6 in.; *Maximum axle load* 17 tons; *Adhesion weight* 49 to 50 tons; *Total locomotive weight* 49 to 50 tons; *Fuel capacity* 330 gal.; *Continuous rated tractive effort and speed* 10,000 lb. at 8 m.p.h.; *Starting tractive effort* 35,000 lb.

EUROPEAN DIESEL-HYDRAULIC SHUNTER: Beginning as the standard diesel shunter of the German Federal Railway, the type has now spread to Belgium, Greece and Turkey, and over 1,000 have been built. Comparatively light locomotive weight in relation to engine power. It was the first standard shunter to have a quick-running diesel engine.

DATA: *Railway* German, Belgian, Turkish, etc.; *Class or name* V.60; *Type* d–h; *Axle arrangement* C; *Built by* Various German and Belgian firms; *Dates built* 1954–68; *No. of engines and h.p.* 1 × 650 b.h.p.; *Engine make* Maybach; *Transmission make* Voith; *Top speed* 37 m.p.h.; *Wheel diameter* 49.2 in.; *Rigid wheelbase* 14 ft. 5 in.; *Total wheelbase* 14 ft. 5 in.; *Maximum axle load* 16.5 to 18.5 tons; *Adhesion weight* 48 to 54 tons; *Total locomotive weight* 48 to 54 tons; *Fuel capacity* 330 gal; *Continuous rated tractive effort and speed* 30,000 lb. at 2.5 m.p.h.

DIESEL ROTARY SNOW PLOUGH: From the first rotary snow plough in 1884 until a few years ago, the cutting and clearing wheels and knives were driven by a reciprocating steam engine, which, with its boiler, was mounted in the snow plough vehicle. This vehicle was pushed at slow speed by one to three steam locomotives. Nowadays, with diesel-hydraulic units, one diesel engine provides both the propulsive power and the cutting-wheel power. Ten-bladed machines like this one, with a cutting-wheel diameter of almost 9 ft., can go at a speed of 2 or 3 m.p.h. through 12 to 15 ft. drifts, and fling the snow 50 to 100 ft. sideways. Ploughs of this type are found today, in Germany, Norway, Sweden and Roumania.

DATA: *Railway* Roumanian State; *Type of power* Diesel-hydraulic; *Number of axles* 4; *Date built* 1966; *Builder* Henschel; *No. of oil engines and h.p.* 1 × 950 b.h.p.; *Engine make* Maybach Mercedes-Benz; *Transmission make* Voith; *Top track speed (running light)* 18 m.p.h.; *Cutting and clearing wheel* 9 ft. diameter, 3 tons weight, maximum speed 160 r.p.m.

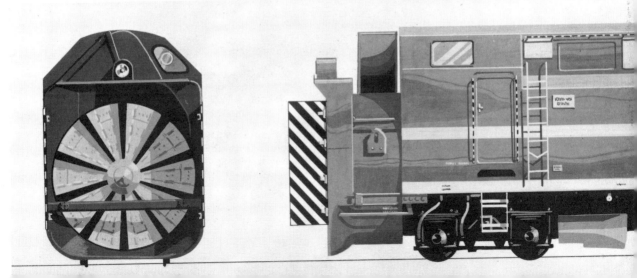

ELECTRIC LOCOMOTIVES

The electric locomotive is not a locomotive at all. Locomotive (and George Stephenson wrote it so in the early days) in essence means "self-moving". The electric locomotive is not self-moving; it does not carry its own power-generating plant as do steam, diesel and gas-turbine locomotives. It is simply a transmitter of power, power that is generated miles away in a central electricity generating station and distributed by miles of cable and overhead wire, and innumerable switchgear plants and substations. A breakdown in any part of that equipment *can* immobilise many electric locomotives, though that does not often occur.

Only because it is merely a transmitter of energy can an electric locomotive be made of high power on moderate weight. On the permissible axle load only transmitting equipment and the vehicle, or running, part have to be carried. So the transmission equipment can be made very powerful. It must give only a little more starting tractive effort than a steam locomotive of equal adhesion weight, otherwise the wheels would slip; but it can carry the tractive effort up to high speeds with comparatively little diminution because of the high h.p. capacity, whereas a steam loco's tractive effort drops off more or less quickly according to the capacity of the boiler. Thus electric locomotives can give very rapid acceleration up to top speed, for they have high h.p. per ton of moving train weight, a very useful factor in railway operation. They can be made to haul heavy freight and passenger trains up steep gradients at the maximum speed permitted by such features as curves, as on the celebrated Gotthard railway. Also it is the power capacity that permits them to run up to very high speeds, for conditions that need, perhaps, 2,500 h.p. at 100 m.p.h. require about 10,000 h.p. at 200 m.p.h., which was approximately the power being developed by the French Bo-Bo locomotive No. 9004 when it attained the world speed record on rails of 205.7 m.p.h. (331 km.p.h.) in March 1955.

Power-wise the electric locomotive comprises only the pantograph or current-collecting apparatus; the switchgear, reverser, and current-transforming equipment (especially with a.c. locomotives), the motors driving the axles, and the driver's controller. But there is a host of auxiliaries and ancillaries such as brake exhausters or compressors, signalling apparatus, force-ventilation blowers to cool motors and transformers, electric brakes, etc. To-day practically all electric locomotives are built as full bogie types, that is, B-B, Bo-Bo, C-C and Co-Co; but some modern types in Europe are able to work under two to four different current types so that they can run across certain frontiers, for in Western Europe there are two a.c. and two d.c. systems all in extensive use.

FRENCH D.C. ELECTRIC LOCOMOTIVE: These were the last big electric locomotives anywhere to be built to old steam locomotive wheel arrangements and on a rigid plate frame; all modern electric locomotives are of double-bogie form. The French
2–Do–2 type began around 1932, and was built in several batches with steadily increasing power until 1950. They formed the
main top-class power on the French 1,500V d.c. system from Paris to Lyons and from Paris to Le Mans until superseded by the
Co-Co locomotives of series 7100 in 1952–53. Each of the four driving axles has one fully-springborne traction motor above
it, but each motor has two armatures, so that in the end over 1,000 h.p. per axle could be given.
DATA: *Railway* French National; *Type of Current* 1,500V d.c.; *Class or no.* 2D2.5300; *Axle arrangement* 2–Do–2; *Built by*
Alsthom; CEM/Fives-Lille; *Dates built* 1933–51; *Rated horse-power* 3,700/4,000; *Top speed* 87 m.p.h.; *Wheel diameter*
67–69 in.; *Rigid wheelbase* 19 ft. 10 in.; *Total wheelbase* 46 ft. 7 in./47 ft. 3 in.; *Maximum axle load* 20 tons; *Total weight*
128/133 tons; *Rated tractive effort and speed* 31,500 lb. at 43 m.p.h.; *Starting tractive effort* 45,000 lb.

BELGIAN HIGH-TENSION D.C. LOCOMOTIVE: This is simply a typical double-bogie medium-power locomotive for the 3,000V d.c. system, with the motor armatures wound for 1,500V d.c., and with series and series-parallel connections. There is nothing special about this class, except perhaps in the control, which has no fewer than 50 notches, and so is very fine. No electric resistance braking is fitted, and locomotive and train are decelerated by air brakes alone. The weight has been taken up to the axle-load limit, so there is sufficient adhesion for the haulage of heavy goods trains.
DATA: *Railway* Belgian National; *Type of current* 3,000V d.c.; *Class or no.* Type 122; *Axle arrangement* Bo–Bo; *Built by* ACEC/Nivelles; *Dates built* 1955–56; *Rated horse-power* 2,500; *Top speed* 77 m.p.h.; *Wheel diameter* 51 in.; *Bogie wheelbase* 11 ft. 4 in.; *Total wheelbase* 39 ft. 6 in.; *Maximum axle load* 20.5 tons; *Adhesion weight* 81 tons; *Total weight* 81 tons; *Rated tractive effort and speed* 31,750 lb. at 30 m.p.h.; *Starting tractive effort* 44,000 lb.

THE LONDON-MERSEYSIDE ELECTRICS: This is the last series of electrics built for British Railways up to 1969, and has detail improvements and greater power than preceding types. These locomotives work the Liverpool and Manchester Pullmans, and many other 78–80 m.p.h. schedules between Euston and Crewe, and run at 95–100 m.p.h. every day. Electric resistance braking is embodied.

DATA: *Railway* British Railways; *Type of current* 25kV 50 cycles single-phase; *Class or no.* AL 6; *Axle arrangement* Bo–Bo; *Built by* Vulcan Foundry, A.E.I.; *Rated horse-power* 3,600 h.p.; *Top speed* 100 m.p.h.; *Wheel diameter* 45 in.; *Bogie wheelbase* 10 ft. 9 in.; *Total wheelbase* 43 ft. 6 in.; *Maximum axle load* 20.3 tons; *Adhesion weight* 81.1 tons; *Total weight* 81.1 tons; *Rated tractive effort and speed* 20,000 lb. at 67 m.p.h.; *Starting tractive effort* 50,000 lb.

8,000 H.P. ELECTRIC FOR 200 KM.P.H.: Newest and most powerful of the German express electrics, the E.03 class was designed specially to run in service at 125 m.p.h., and for the few stretches on which this rate is permitted special continuous visible signalling and brake control is fitted. Through runs of more than 500 miles are made with high-speed passenger trains. Electric resistance braking and a 39-notch thyristor control system are included.

DATA: *Railway* German Federal; *Type of current* 15kV 16.6 cycles single-phase; *Class or no.* E.03; *Axle arrangement* Co-Co; *Built by* Henschel, Siemens; *Dates built* 1965–66, 1970; *Rated horse-power* 8,000 h.p.; *Top speed* 125 m.p.h.; *Wheel diameter* 49 in.; *Bogie wheelbase* 14 ft. 9 in.; *Total wheelbase* 46 ft. 4 in.; *Maximum axle load* 19 tons; *Adhesion weight* 112 tons; *Total weight* 112 tons; *Rated tractive effort and speed* 24,000 lb. at 125 m.p.h.; *Starting tractive effort* 70,000 lb.

GERMAN STANDARD EXPRESS ELECTRIC: About one-quarter of the whole West German railway system is electrified on the old single-phase system with current at 16.6 cycles, but it carries nearly three-quarters of the total traffic. Something like 90 per cent of the electric traffic is handled by four standard classes of locomotives, of which the E.10 type, shown here, is the most powerful of the four-axle models. Some are geared for 75 and 87 m.p.h. top speed, but a few for 100 m.p.h.

DATA: *Railway* German Federal; *Type of current* 15kV 16.6 cycles single-phase; *Class or no.* E.10; *Axle arrangement* Bo–Bo; *Built by* Henschel, Krauss-Maffei Siemens, Brown Boveri; *Dates built* 1955–66; *Rated horse-power* 4,850; *Top speed* 87 m.p.h. (E.10); 100 m.p.h. (E.101); *Wheel diameter* 49.5 in.; *Bogie wheelbase* 11ft 2 in.; *Total wheelbase* 37ft.; *Maximum axle load* 21 tons; *Adhesion weight* 83 tons; *Total weight* 83 tons; *Rated tractive effort and speed* 23,800 lb. at 75 m.p.h.; *Starting tractive effort* 45,000 lb.

SWISS "GOTTHARD" LOCOMOTIVES: These are often known as the Gotthard locomotives, for they were built specially to haul the heaviest passenger and goods trains over that mountain line, which has many spirals and 180-degree loops and a long ruling gradient of 1 in 37 on each side of the 9.3-mile summit tunnel. The sharp curves limit the speed to 37 m.p.h. (60 km. p.h.) over part of the route; but the Co–Co locomotives have to be able to maintain this as a minimum with 600/650-ton passenger trains and 800-ton freight trains, and to start these trains on the 1 in 37 and accelerate them up to the rated speed.

DATA: *Railway* Swiss Federal; *Type of current* 15kV 16.6 cycle single-phase; *Class or no.* 1400; *Axle arrangement* Co–Co; *Built by* S. L. M./Brown Boveri; *Dates built* 1952-66; *Rated horse-power* 6,000 h.p.; *Top speed* 78 m.p.h.; *Wheel diameter* 49.6 in.; *Bogie wheelbase* 14 ft. 1¾ in.; *Total wheelbase* 42 ft. 7¾ in.; *Maximum axle load* 21 tons; *Adhesion weight* 122.5 tons; *Total weight* 122.5 tons; *Rated tractive effort and speed* 46,700 lb. at 46 m.p.h.; *Starting tractive effort* 72,000 lb.

FRENCH QUADRI-CURRENT ELECTRICS: This is a high-power high-speed locomotive of extreme flexibility in operation, for it has alternate reduction gears (which can be changed by the driver with the locomotive at standstill) that permit of top speeds of either 100 or 150 m.p.h. (the latter for the future); and it can operate over four different current systems. Two of these, 1,500V d.c. and 25kV 50 cycles single-phase, are to suit the two systems operated by the French National Railways; the other two are to suit the neighbouring Belgian (d.c.) and German and Swiss (single-phase) Federal Railways.

DATA: *Railway* French National; *Type of current* 25kV 50 cycles single-phase, 15kV 16.6 cycles, single-phase, 3,000V direct current, 1,500V direct current; *Class or no.* 40100; *Axle arrangement* C–C; *Built by* Alsthom; *Dates built* 1965–66; *Rated horse-power* 5,150; *Top speed* 100 and 150 m.p.h.; *Wheel diameter* 43.5 in.; *Bogie wheelbase (monomotor bogie)* 10 ft. 8 in.; *Total wheelbase* 58 ft.; *Maximum axle load* 17 tons; *Adhesion weight* 102 tons; *Total weight* 102 tons.

INDEX